# Without Reservations

*Happy Holidays From the Gang*

# Without Reservations

An Uncensored, Unabashed Look
At How People Behave In Hotels

*Fred V. Alias*
Editor-in-Chief

*WITHOUT RESERVATIONS*
An Uncensored Unabashed Look
at How People Behave in Hotels
*Fred V. Alias, Editor-in-Chief*

Printed and bound by Haddon Craftsmen, Inc.,
Scranton, Pennsylvania

Dustjacket and book design by
Robert Howard Graphic Design
Fort Collins, Colorado

96 95 94 93     5 4 3 2

ISBN  0-9633894-3-2

Library of Congress Catalog Card Number: 92-64283

## Dedication

To George ("Lightnin'") Falls, the main reason I joined Holiday Inn hotels. I was interested in a public relations career, but George said the only thing available was a position in sales. I'll never forget his saying "Look — let's just get you on the train. We'll find you a seat once we get going."

To my assistant, Joanne Love, who always starts my day on an up beat, 364 days a year...she takes Christmas off!

To my parents, who taught me one of the greatest values of all — tenacity.

To my wife, Becky, and my children, Shaler, Alden, Andrew and Hillyer. No matter what direction life takes you, you're sure to have ups and downs. And, the best way to survive them is to laugh. Even if it means laughing at yourself. Life makes no sense with no sense of humor.

Fred V. Alias, 1992

# Introduction

*F*irst as an employee and then as a Holiday Inn hotels franchisee for the past 25 years, I have been amused, delighted, shocked, and just plain fascinated by the way people conduct themselves in hotels. I think the people are what kept me interested in this business.

Something happens to people when they check into a hotel. Maybe it's the welcome escape from everyday life, basking in the luxury of crisp, clean sheets everyday, not to mention unlimited clean towels. To know that you're sheltered and protected 24 hours a day, with an entire staff at your beck and call. To have cookies and milk brought to you at bedtime. The whole experience almost conjures up a silent declaration: "I am special and life is good."

Hotels are such a big part of the human experience and I wondered why there is so little written about hotels and the people who stay in them. Everyone has heard an outrageous tale or two about the characters in our business — the frazzled bellhop, frenzied waitress, peculiar people, enchanting children, cranky seniors, unclad bodies locked out of their rooms, bizarre "family" pets. The list goes on and on.

*Then it struck me.*

Wouldn't it be great if someone compiled a collection of the best from the best — favorite stories of the people who know their guests so well. The employees of Holiday Inn hotels. They're very people-driven; they really do care. If anything were to happen, they would know. And, they would remember.

I mentioned this idea in a meeting one day with J. Raymond Lewis, Holiday Inn Worldwide Senior Vice President of Marketing. In his wisdom, Ray immediately saw its merits and suggested we use it to commemorate the 40th Anniversary of Holiday Inns, Inc.

So, together, we mapped out a plan to gather stories from Holiday Inn hotels throughout the land.

*And, the response was extraordinary.*

Anecdotes by the hundreds. A wealth of human experience. Moments in time, indelibly etched in the minds of our staff. Everything from drama, suspense and danger, to warmth and laughs. Lots and lots of laughs.

I suspect there may be a strong correlation between the caring attitude we've always encouraged and the fact that we are the largest, most successful hotel company in the world.

So, for the hotel renowned for guarding guest privacy with a passion, please allow us this one indiscretion, so that we may share with the rest of the world this loving glimpse of human nature, at its

*unpredictable,*
*inconceivable,*
*unforgettable*
*best.*

# Table of Contents

# CHAPTER ONE

A t Your Service

# Now that's fresh

Our elegant restaurant opens onto the Holidome, providing a lush tropical setting, complete with flowing fountain and a pond stocked with goldfish. In addition to our pet macaw, Popeye, this setting is home to several birds.

One evening, I was summoned to the dining room at the insistence of a distinguished guest. She rose, shook my hand vigorously and praised the hotel on so grandly fulfilling the menu's promise. Then, with a flourish, she lifted the napkin on her plate to reveal a small goldfish flopping around on her plate.

As I stood speechless, she explained that just moments after she had ordered the fresh fish entree, a bird swooped down, as if on cue, and deposited the goldfish on her plate!

# What a darling nightlite

❧ ❧ ❧ ❧ ❧ ❧ ❧ ❧ ❧

*W*e are all aware that today's society not only looks for bigger and better, but also faster, shinier and who has the most buttons. To this end, the hotel industry is no slouch. We have facsimile machines for instant mail, copiers for immediate reproductions, computers for instantaneous calculations, information and record keeping.

In short, if there is a new, improved way of doing something or a gadget that will make our guests' stay more enjoyable, hotels will take the lead. This is also what our guests have come to expect at Holiday Inn hotels.

One of our recent guests, a diminutive, elderly Southern Belle, was settling her account at the Front Desk prior to departure. She told me it had been quite a while since she had done any traveling and continued to say how much she had enjoyed her stay with us. Everyone had been so friendly. The Hotel was so pleasant. The restaurant had been wonderful. But she was most impressed with the modern conveniences, especially the darling little red blinking light on the telephone so she could find it at night in the dark.

I thanked her and wished her well. But, I never did tell her the item that had most impressed her was the message light. I simply smiled and gave her the telephone message.

# Tall dark and handsome

❧ ❧ ❧ ❧ ❧ ❧ ❧ ❧ ❧

*O*n a rather quiet afternoon, we got a call for Room Service. A very pleasant lady ordered a hamburger and soft drink. And then, jokingly asked to have "someone tall, dark and handsome" bring it up to her.

Having been trained to treat the guest's every whim as command, I promptly enlisted the help of our chef. You see, our chef is 6'7" tall, exceedingly good looking and has a golden brown complexion...and a great sense of humor.

Moments after he gallantly delivered the order, the lady called back. Laughing so hard she could barely express her thanks.

# Just like home!

❧ ❧ ❧ ❧ ❧ ❧ ❧ ❧ ❧

*A* Priority Club member remembers Margaret, a head waitress who truly understands what customer service means...

I stay at a Holiday Inn hotel in Virginia approximately 30 nights per year. Over the years, I have built some great relationships with the people there. One of my favorites is Margaret.

At breakfast one morning, I was placing my order of sausage and eggs. I asked why no link sausage was available, to which she replied: "Nobody ever asks for it." When I expressed my disappointment, she asked how long I would be staying in the hotel. I told her two more days and she went on to serve my breakfast.

The following morning, I placed my usual order for sausage and eggs. Margaret delivered my breakfast within minutes. And, lo and behold! There were the eggs, surrounded by link sausage!

Needless to say, I was delighted. When I asked how this had happened, Margaret smiled and told me "I brought them from home, just for you!" And, she brought plenty, for the next morning's breakfast included link sausage.

Being treated as a valued customer by people who really care is what keeps bringing me back to Holiday Inn hotels. Thanks, Margaret!

# Now hear this

*One* night during the Persian Gulf War, I was working late in my office when the Front Desk called for Maintenance on the walkie-talkie. Knowing that my night Engineer was busy, I took the call.

The request was from a guest visiting her son before his naval unit was to ship out to the Gulf. She complained of a high-pitched noise coming from somewhere in her room. Entering the room, I found her going through a stack of mail on her bed. We both listened intently, but could hear nothing. I told her to call me again if it recurred.

Seconds after I returned to my office, she called. But a second inspection — from the closet to the plumbing — revealed nothing.

Finally, after her third call, I rushed to the room in time to hear the mysterious noise — the familiar strains of "Anchors Aweigh!" The old Navy standard was coming from her stack of mail. Quickly she sorted through the unopened envelopes to find a musical Mother's Day card from her second son — a sailor already serving in the Gulf!

# No nudes is good nudes

ઠ ઠ ઠ ઠ ઠ ઠ ઠ ઠ ઠ

One sultry, southern summer night, approaching midnight, the hotel switchboard lit up in a ringing frenzy. Giggling voices alerted me to the presence of a skinny dipper at the pool. Assuring each caller — especially the senior ladies' tour group — that the impromptu Late Show would soon be ended, I scurried to the pool, armed with my trusty flashlight.

The silhouette of a bare man glistened in the moonlight. Now, how was I, a demure female Manager, going to handle this situation?

As I crept closer, the guests watched from their windows. There he was! With a wit far better endowed than his physique, he stood, posing as if in a body builder's meet, boasting "I suppose you've come to watch, too!"

Like the marshal in an olde time Western, I felt obliged to use my weapon. With a strategic flick of my flashlight and a quick comment, the flasher fled.

Next morning at checkout, the twenty ladies were bursting with curiosity. How had I convinced him to leave so abruptly?

"Oh, I merely told him we have certain standards for entertainment at the Holiday Inn hotel," I replied. "And his show simply came up short!"

# No shoes, no shirt, no service

❧ ❧ ❧ ❧ ❧ ❧ ❧ ❧ ❧

One evening in our cocktail lounge, a rather flamboyant female patron decided to offer her own floor show.

Taking a seat at the bar, she began to slowly extricate herself from her clothing. She kicked off her shoes and slipped off her jacket. She slowly unbuttoned her blouse and for the grand finale, let her wraparound skirt fall to the floor. As she sat back. In all her glory!

The bartender could take no more and went running for help. He corralled the diminutive female Director of Sales in the hallway. Unsure how to handle the situation, she stepped up to the naked patron and calmly said, "Pardon me, Ma'am. I'm afraid you'll have to leave. You see, we have a strict policy at the Holiday Inn hotel — No Shoes, No Service!"

# Buckle up!

*a a a a a a a a a*

*I*n 1983, while working for an engineering consulting firm, four young men were assigned to a project in North Carolina. Lodging was provided at the local Holiday Inn hotel. It was a paradise for this road group, because it had not one, but two lounges!

Having been in town for about two weeks, the group was sitting at the bar in the smaller lounge downstairs. After several hours of shooting the breeze, WHAM! One of the fellows leaned back on his barstool and fell. Flat on his back. Still on the stool.

Well, needless to say he rose to a warm round of applause and cheers. Took a bow and mumbled something about his three comrades under his breath. The bartender told him she would have to cut him off and the group bid all a "Good Night!" and retired to their rooms.

The next evening, the four guys headed for the lounge. Settling into their usual barstools, they placed their orders. Suddenly, the bartender walked around the bar and stepped behind the fellow who'd fallen. She offered to buckle him in...Somewhere she'd found a set of seat belts and attached them to his stool. Just in case he "flipped" again that night!

# Oh, so you know my Dad...

☙ ☙ ☙ ☙ ☙ ☙ ☙ ☙ ☙

*T*he vivacious and very attractive daughter of our Hotel's owner was hired as a Front Desk clerk for the summer. Like many college students, she was very friendly. Unlike some college students, however, she was also very sophisticated.

One evening, a distinguished middle-aged gentleman entered the Lobby and checked in. He asked if the young Desk Clerk would join him for a cocktail. She demurely declined, saying management did not allow such behavior of staff members. He asked what time she went off duty. She replied, "11:00 p.m., sir." He asked if she would join him in the lounge after her shift ended. She politely explained that management did not allow employees to fraternize with guests. He smugly told her not to worry. He was meeting with the Hotel's owner the next morning and would square things for her at that time...

The lovely young Clerk smiled sweetly and said, "Oh! I wouldn't do that if I were you, Sir. The Hotel's owner is my father."

# The walls have ears...and legs ...and arms.

&&&&&&&&&

One day, the Room Attendant was doing a routine check of vacant guest rooms. She noticed a loose tile in the bathroom ceiling and attempted to reset it properly. As she struggled with the unwieldy tile, something popped out.

Something bigger than life.

A box, stored in the ceiling, fell open. She pulled out its contents to reveal an inflatable doll. A life-size inflatable doll. The Housekeeper then realized why a certain traveling salesman always returned to the same room.

Following procedure, she turned the item over to the Executive Housekeeper for Lost and Found Storage. Where it remains to this day.

# Squeaky clean intentions

≈ ≈ ≈ ≈ ≈ ≈ ≈ ≈ ≈

*F*or several weeks, the Maintenance Department had been receiving complaints from a variety of guests. The doors to their rooms squeaked when they were opened or closed.

For each complaint, we'd go to the room; pull the pins out of the door hinges, lubricate them and put them back up. This cured the problem. But the same symptoms were reported in more and more rooms. Finally, my boss had had enough. One slow day, he said to me, "I want you to lubricate every door hinge in this building!"

I proceeded to embark on this sizable task. By midafternoon, I was rapidly working my way down the hallway of the third floor. Things were going well. Most of the rooms were vacant since it was past checkout time, but just to be sure, I always knock first before entering with my passkey.

When I got to room 306, I knocked as usual and was about to use my key, when the door flew open. Standing there was a woman in her night-gown, impatiently waiting for an explanation.

Startled, I nervously blurted out, "Lady, uh, Hi. Uh, I've come to grease your hinges."

She obviously misunderstood my intentions, for she swung her hand hard across my face, knocking me off balance. Being small of stature, it was several moments before I recovered from the blow and was able to explain — in a better way — why I was there. When she finally understood, she was most apologetic and even gave me a big hug. And I got to fix her door, of course.

That incident happened many years ago, but to this day, whenever I have reason to knock on a guest's door, I take two steps back and wait...

# *And behind door number 2...*

*A* gentleman checked in late one night. He had spent the day traveling and was understandably exhausted. He headed straight to bed.

About 6 a.m., our guest got up to go to the bathroom. Not ready to be fully awakened, he stumbled along without turning on the lights. As in many hotels, our bathroom door is located adjacent to the front hallway door of the room. You guessed it — he chose the wrong door!

Standing in the brightly lit hallway, he heard the loud click of the door lock as it closed behind him. Our frantic guest (who dislikes pajamas), was stuck in the hallway without a stitch of clothing. Needless to say, he felt pressured to rectify the situation...and fast

Unfortunately, the possibilities were limited. The only item in sight was a small pink napkin on a recently finished breakfast tray. Our guest seized the moment...and the napkin!

In the tradition of Tarzan and other brave adventurers, our guest made a makeshift loincloth of the napkin. He jumped on the elevator and pushed the emergency button. Security came to the rescue and managed to correct the situation with a straight face.

Our guest was extremely embarrassed, but we all thought he covered the situation very well!

# Where's the maintenance man when you need him...

❧ ❧ ❧ ❧ ❧ ❧ ❧ ❧ ❧

*T*he Hotel was buzzing. Full occupancy. Kids running through the lobby. People checking in. Phones ringing off the hook. Just another day at the Holiday Inn hotel. Then the Front Desk received a call reporting someone stuck in the elevator.

Within seconds, the maintenance man was paged. No response. Another page. And again. The staff searched the guest room floors and then the Hotel grounds. Thirty minutes went by. Still no maintenance man.

We were growing more and more anxious for the poor guest in the elevator, who was probably desperate and wondering if he'd ever be rescued by our staff.

All the while, the Front Desk Clerk kept calling the phone in the elevator to reassure the unfortunate guest. But, there was no answer! Things were really getting strange.

Finally, 45 long minutes later, the elevator came back to life. The drama built as the doors slowly opened...to reveal — the maintenance man!

(Later we learned the elevator phone had a loose wire, which is why he was there in the first place. In addition to not hearing it ring, he couldn't use it to call out to answer his page(s)!)

# You've lost that holiday feeling

≈ ≈ ≈ ≈ ≈ ≈ ≈ ≈ ≈

Summer of '76. It was our nation's Bicentennial. Many families were visiting Washington D.C. to celebrate the country's 200th birthday. Holiday Inn hotels new theme song was all the rage. "You Get That Holiday Feeling at Holiday Inn."

It was late at night. We'd checked in our umpteenth guest and were enthusiastically practicing our "Holiday Feeling" routine. Our carefully choreographed routine consisted of a young desk clerk between two male employees. We sang to the lyrics to our popular theme song, kicking our legs to the left, turning and kicking to the right.

Imagine our chagrin when we realized we had an audience!

A dusty station wagon had pulled into the front driveway. The weary driver, his wife, five small children and large family dog stared at us, wide-eyed. Then drove away into the night.

Our theatrical careers in tatters, we never performed our routine again. But we often wondered what became of the family who didn't get that Holiday feeling!

# You what?!

≈a ≈a ≈a ≈a ≈a ≈a ≈a ≈a ≈a

Our General Manager was contacted by an out-
raged guest. It seems the Housekeeper had thrown
away THREE pairs of his shoes. Prompt inquiry
revealed, however, that the shoes (which looked
old and tattered) were in the trash can and the
hapless Housekeeper thought the guest intended to
throw them out.

The indignant guest informed the General
Manager, he ALWAYS placed his shoes in the trash
can! And, we should train our Housekeepers not to
empty them!

# You can't get good help anymore

ex ex ex ex ex ex ex ex ex

*O*ur Hotel was filled to the max when one of the worst ice storms ever hit our area. The weather was so bad that only two people from the Housekeeping Department were able to make it to work.

A famous Country & Western singer, along with his band, occupied six rooms. They'd been with us for some time and we considered them part of the family. The band members offered to help clean the rooms. Of course, we declined their offer at first. But, as time went on, the rooms were not getting cleaned fast enough. We relented and took them up on their offer.

These guys jumped right in. They worked along side us as if they were at home and just helping out. After a few hours, I began to feel better about getting the job done.

I was so exhausted that I did not notice that my "helper" had disappeared. As I fluffed the pillows, I noticed this guy standing in the doorway with a blank look on his face.

I said, "Don't just stand there. Go get some more towels!"

He asked, "Where are they?"

Giving him directions, I wondered how he could have forgotten so quickly where the laundry was. When he returned, I told him to place them on the cart. Suddenly, I realized this man was a perfect stranger. He wasn't my helper! I asked him what room he was staying in...

With a grin, he replied, "Ma'am, I just checked in. And, this is my room...I think!"

# Dress for success

ã ã ã ã ã ã ã ã ã

After working nine years in the restaurant, I wish I'd kept a journal. So many funny things happen every day...it's hard to remember them all. One of my favorite stories involves a young waitress on the early morning shift. She always seemed to be getting ready for work as she walked through the door.

One morning, she was running late and when she got here, we were already busy. So, she grabbed a pencil and her tickets and started taking orders.

All at once, everyone in the restaurant burst into laughter.

Right on the top of her head was a big pink roller!

Needless to say, she now gets up a little earlier to get ready for work.

# Stay with someone you know

*ⵣ ⵣ ⵣ ⵣ ⵣ ⵣ ⵣ ⵣ ⵣ*

*W*hile steadily working the Front Desk, a lady called, in much distress.

"How may I help you?" I asked with concern.

"I'm looking for Mrs. Bell. Is she registered at your Hotel?"

When I said "No, ma'am," she became distraught.

In a trembling voice, she cried, "You see, I'm Mrs. Bell. I am she. And, I am lost. Lost as can be. I checked into one of your fine Hotels, you see. When I left my room, I took my key. I took the shuttle bus to enjoy the sights. Now I am lost. Do I go left or right?"

By now she was crying and begging for help. Alone in a phone booth with no change left. I took down the number and told her to stop crying, things would be fine. "We'll find your Hotel and call you in no time."

One Hotel. Two Hotels. Three's the charm! I found her Hotel. Oh, gosh. Oh, darn!

This story is true, though poorly told. It just goes to show. When traveling, "Stay...with someone you know!"

# Keep your pants on!

ᴥ ᴥ ᴥ ᴥ ᴥ ᴥ ᴥ ᴥ ᴥ

*I*t was late winter, 1980. I had just finished working a 12 hour shift at the Front Desk. I went up to my room and took my pants off to relax. As I sat there in the dark, I looked out my window. It had been snowing for several hours and everything was covered in a thick blanket of snow.

Then, I noticed a car with four seasoned ladies coming towards the Hotel. The only problem was, their car was heading straight for the in-ground pool. Due to a fire, the pool did not have a fence around it and with all the snow, it was impossible to see. I ran screaming out of my room. Waving my arms, I finally managed to stop the ladies, just short of the pool.

When they realized I had saved them they were grateful; however, the driver suggested that next time, I should keep my pants on!

It seems that I was in such a big hurry to help these ladies, I'd forgotten to put my pants back on...so all they saw was a man running around in the parking lot screaming. Waving his arms. In his underwear in freezing weather!

# Can we please check out?

*A* short time after we opened in 1963, an inno-
cent young couple rented the bridal suite. The next
morning, I saw the honeymooners in the lobby.
They looked nervous and upset. I asked if I could
help.

The young man said they were planning to
meet someone for lunch, but the sign in the room
stated that check out time was 12 noon. If they
had to wait until noon to check out, they would be
late for their lunch date. He wanted to know if
there was any way they could leave before noon!

Of course, I explained the purpose of posting
check out times and assured him they could leave
at any time. He thanked me profusely and they
went merrily on their way

# Mr. Sandman

ða ða ða ða ða ða ða ða ða

$S$everal years ago, the early morning crew came to work as usual at 6:00 a.m. Snow was in the forecast, but little did we know what was in the making. By lunchtime, we were caught in a blizzard. By the end of lunch, we were fully aware that the morning crew was not going home because the afternoon and evening crews were not going to make it in!

The Front Desk was swamped with check-ins and requests for rooms. Our General Manager blocked a few rooms for the crew and the rest were sold in no time. People started to share rooms, even with strangers. They doubled, tripled and in some cases, even quadrupled! We realized we had a real snow emergency on our hands.

Our Hotel was filled to capacity and people kept streaming in. Our restaurant was the only one in town that had not closed. With Chef's speedy crew, we organized a "Snowdrift Buffet" and every employee — no matter what department — assisted in the Dining Room. We fed several hundred people. They sat wherever they could find a chair and ate what we had to offer.

It was past midnight when we closed the Dining Room. We had people sleeping on cots in the meeting rooms, in the lobby, and even in the Concierge Room. I was happy to know there was a room blocked for us as we readied the Dining Room for the 6:00 a.m. breakfast buffet.

It was well past 2:00 a.m. when we were finally able to go to our assigned sleeping room. When we got to the room, however, the door was wide open and our Concierge was sitting in the corner, reading a magazine. As we proceeded into the room, we recognized one of our regular customers — sprawled out across the bed, snoring loudly! The Concierge explained very calmly that the customer could not get home and had wanted to take a short "cat nap" because he was very tired. She offered our room to him, until we needed it, but unfortunately, we were unable to wake him up. So, the four of us went back to the Dining Room and had our own cat naps — in a booth!

# CHAPTER TWO

# Are We Speaking the Same Language???

❧ ❧ ❧ ❧ ❧ ❧ ❧ ❧ ❧ ❧ ❧ ❧

# *Just how far do you want to go?*

❧ ❧ ❧ ❧ ❧ ❧ ❧ ❧ ❧

*A*s a recent emigre from Scotland, I was getting quite an education about life in America while working as Night Auditor for the Holiday Inn hotel of North Platte, Nebraska.

One relatively quiet night, the Front Desk phone rang at about 2:00 a.m. As I answered, the male caller abruptly inquired: "What does it take to get a broad in this town?"

English being my second language, I had never heard this expression other than in the context of traveling. So, in all sincerity, I replied, "Oh, I doubt it would be possible tonight, sir. But, you could call your friendly local travel agent in the morning and assuming you have a valid passport, they could send you abroad."

After a long pause, the caller hung up.

# *It's only good for cold cash*

Our Front Desk received an irate phone call from a member of an international airline crew, who was very upset and demanded to see the Manager.

It seems all the food and drinks he had stored in his room's refrigerator were spoiled because the 'fridge was obviously out of order.

Our diplomatic General Manager very carefully explained to the red-faced guest that the "refrigerator" was actually a wall safe!

# *Just what did you have in mind?*

❧ ❧ ❧ ❧ ❧ ❧ ❧ ❧ ❧

*T*o improve efficiency, Room Attendants often remove bedsheets from several rooms before making the beds. With that in mind, consider this actual conversation:

*(KNOCK, KNOCK)*

*Attendant:* "Housekeeping"

*Guest (opening door):* "Yes?"

*Attendant:* "May I come in and strip?"

*Delighted guest:* "By all means! How much time do you need?"

*Attendant:* "Oh, 15 minutes or so."

*Ever-more delighted guest:* "Uh...how much do you make?"

*Attendant:* "Oh, just a regular wage."

*Guest who feels he won the sweepstakes:* "Really? Well, maybe you can stay longer."

*Attendant:* "Oh no, I couldn't...I have other guests to service."

# Does that come in a spray or just a pump?

ə ə ə ə ə ə ə ə ə

*O*ccasionally, the famous "generation gap" rears its ugly head.

We were having a meeting, with cleanliness as the main topic. The senior Housekeeping shift leader mentioned how important it was for Room Attendants to use a little "elbow grease."

Several young workers exchanged puzzled glances and immediately asked what brand this new chemical was. They couldn't recall ever having seen it advertised!

# The happy hookers

28 28 28 28 28 28 28 28 28

*L*ike many Holiday Inn hotels, we have a large marquee at our property on which we often display friendly greetings to our incoming groups.

Well, you had to be there a couple of years ago to believe the number of men who stopped by or called, asking about a knitting club we were hosting...how long they'd be there...and how much they charged for their services.

You see, the name of the knitting group was "The Happy Hookers" and our clever marquee message read: "Welcome, Hookers!"

# When in Rome, say "Achoo"

*An eager waiter in our restaurant was, with the expected flourish, adding freshly ground pepper to a guest's salad.

The international guest, in an animated fashion, kept asking for more, shouting "Faster! Faster!"

The waiter continued to grind.

Until a nearby, bilingual patron pointed out that the man was Italian and was shouting "Bosta! Bosta!" (Translated: "Stop! Stop!")

# Just following procedure, Sir

𝕒 𝕒 𝕒 𝕒 𝕒 𝕒 𝕒 𝕒 𝕒

*T*he staff of any Hotel is made up of a wide variety of people. The differences range from gender and religious beliefs to race and age. Sometimes included are people with special needs.

Our Hotel was very actively involved with an organization which helped locate positions for immigrants with limited or no comprehension of the English language. We used translators during the first two weeks training period and then the employee was expected to follow the same work ethic as any other employee. Most of the training was done by rote — an established method or procedure performed exactly the same way each and every time.

Our newest immigrant employee was a Room Attendant. She had been taught to approach a room, knock on the door, announce "Housekeeping" and proceed to clean the room. All went well during training and for the first few weeks thereafter...

Until, that is, the Front Desk received a frantic phone call from one of the guestrooms. The Room Attendant had followed procedure exactly. Unfortunately, we had not foreseen one variable.

The Room Attendant approached the room. She knocked. She announced. She entered...and began stripping the bed. What we had failed to teach her was that no one was supposed to be in the bed when removing the linen!

# How do you say Dubonnet?

&a &a &a &a &a &a &a &a &a

*W*hile working in a Holiday Inn hotel Restaurant, you come into contact with many ethnic groups and varied accents, guests as well as employees.

My story is about Johnny, our youngest Hispanic busboy.

Every year, our restaurant crew gets together for a Christmas party. We draw names and exchange small gifts. Early in December, Johnny picked Sue's name out of the hat. Sue is our longest working waitress and quite a character herself. For the next few weeks, Sue hinted to Johnny that she would love a bottle of Dubonnet...

The day of the party arrived. Everyone began exchanging gifts. A very shy Johnny approached Sue, with an alternate gift and a little speech: "Susie, Susie. I go everywhere. I go uptown. I go downtown. Dis Dubonnet eez no perfume!"

# What did you say?

ta ta ta ta ta ta ta ta ta

*A* couple of years ago we had an incident which proved the need for more effective English education for our Spanish-speaking employees.

"Pedro" is a top notch employee. A dedicated Room Server for our restaurant, he has been nominated Employee of the Month many times and was Employee of the Year in 1991.

On one occasion, however, we received a complaint that he was making untoward advances to a female guest. She identified Pedro by name and said, "He came into my Room and sat on my bed. When I asked him to leave, he said 'see you tonight!'"

Unable to believe we were hearing this about our star employee, we questioned Pedro. "Did you sit on her bed?" we demanded.

In his broken English, Pedro replied: "Si. She tell me to sit it on the bed. So I sit on the bed." Pedro did not know the difference between sit and set.

When we asked him about wanting to see the guest later that evening, he replied: "Oh, yes! I always say this. In Espanol, we say Buenos Noches! In English, 'See you tonight!' I no say this?" We informed Pedro of his correct thinking, but wrong choice of words.

We called the guest and explained that Pedro was not well-versed in English. He had misinterpreted her request to set the tray on the bed. We also explained that when Pedro said "see you tonight" he thought it was the equivalent of "Have a good evening or see you later."

Of course, once the guest understood the miscommunication, she laughed. For that matter, we all had a good laugh.

# He did. Did she?

🙙 🙙 🙙 🙙 🙙 🙙 🙙 🙙 🙙

*D*uring all the years I have worked at the Front
Desk, I have met all types of people. But, one
couple always comes to mind when the subject of
funny stories is brought up.

One day, a middle-aged couple checked in
and requested a Room near the lobby. They made
it clear no other location would do. Of course, we
try to please all of our customers, so we gave them
a Room near the lobby. They settled in and everything was fine. Or was it?

Moments after the band started playing in the
lounge, the phone at the Front Desk started ringing. It was the woman in the Room near the lobby.
She was terribly upset. She insisted we move them
to another Room. The band was too loud. But, it
was late. The Hotel was full and there was not
another Room available. She slammed down the
receiver.

A short while later, the woman called the
Front Desk again and demanded to see the Manager. The Night Manager went to the Room. After
several minutes of conversation, the lady agreed to
stay and try to forget the situation. We were relieved and felt the rest of the night would go by
smoothly.

We were wrong. The woman walked through
the lobby and headed for the lounge. She ordered a

drink and asked to speak with the Manager of the lounge. She argued with him and insisted that the band should stop playing and be asked to leave. Of course, this was not possible and she retired to her much-hated Room.

Finally, at 2 a.m. the Lounge closed. The band went home. And we didn't see the woman again.

Early the next morning, the woman and her husband came to the Front Desk to check out. The man was in good spirits and couldn't say enough about their accommodations. He was full of compliments. He thought the Room was pleasant and comfortable. The service was outstanding. It was the best night's sleep he'd had in weeks! He would like the same Room when they came back to stay with us in the future.

We were overwhelmed. It was hard to believe that these two people had shared the same room. Guess this story explains the expression "You can please some people all of the time, but you can't please all of the people, all of the time."

# Was that 1800 or 0600?

❧ ❧ ❧ ❧ ❧ ❧ ❧ ❧ ❧

*I* was working the Front Desk on the 3-11 p.m. shift. The phone rang. It was one of our regular guests. He wanted to know why he hadn't received his 6:00 o'clock wake up call. He insisted that his four co-workers had taken the only car they shared and had left for work without him. He demanded that I supply him with transportation to his work site, which was 17 miles away.

Checking my call sheet for the evening, I couldn't find his name. I thought we'd really goofed. Sure enough, there was his name...on the call sheet for the next morning. What could have happened?!

Well. It turns out that the guest had come in after a hard day, laid down for a moment and fallen asleep. When he woke up it was 6:30 and he thought he'd slept through the night. Hurrying to dress for work, he looked in the parking lot. The car was gone. He thought he'd been left behind. And, was he annoyed!

Of course, as darkness fell, we were able to convince him it wasn't morning at all. His co-workers had gone out to dinner, not to work. When they heard his story, they nicknamed him "AM/PM" and to this day, every time he checks in, we all have a great laugh.

# *So much in common*

❧ ❧ ❧ ❧ ❧ ❧ ❧ ❧ ❧

*O*n Tuesday evenings, our lobby is the site of the General Manager's Happy Hour — an opportunity for our management staff to meet and greet clients over complimentary cocktails and hors d'oeuvres.

We host travelers from all over the world and on one occasion a guest named Sally, a sweet young lass, was introduced to one of our international guests named Sahedas.

"So, Mr. Sahedas," says Sally. "Where are you from?"

"I am from Persia," he replied.

"Oh, really!" gushed Sally. "That's where my cat is from!"

# East meets West

ta ta ta ta ta ta ta ta ta

*A* Priority Club member was living in residence at
the Holiday Inn, Juhu Beach, Bombay INDIA approximately twelve months when the following
anecdote occurred.

His room had become his home away from
home, thanks to the wonderful people — the
chambermaids, the bellmen, the waiters and beautiful waitresses and Front Desk clerks, especially the
telephone switchboard operators. They all contrib-
uted to make his stay in India a treasured memory.

One bright sunny day, business required that
he travel by rail from Bombay to North Central
India, a distance in excess of fifteen hundred kilo-
meters. Eighteen hours riding the rails. One way.

His business completed after several days, he
returned to Bombay, via the same railroad line.
The return trip required nineteen hours. Arriving
at the Hotel, the weary businessman looked for-
ward to a nice soak in the large bath and a long
night's rest between the clean, crisp sheets of his
king size bed.

Along about 2 a.m., however, he awakened to
find numerous visitors in bed with him...uninvited
visitors. The bed was crawling with bugs and the
man came unglued. He routed out the staff...The
entire staff responded and the bed was removed
from the room within seconds. The room was

vacuumed in minutes and not a bug remained — except for one. He carried on like a madman, the classic "Ugly American" accusing the management and staff of causing the invasion. Finally having vented his anger, he fell exhausted into bed and retired for the night.

The next morning, the beautiful sales Manager visited the businessman to review the situation. Having lived in the room for nearly twelve months without an incident involving "bugs" it became apparent in short order that the "visitors" had been picked up during the railroad ride back to Bombay, Coach Third Class. They'd "hitched a ride" from the interior of India via his luggage and books.

It would be an understatement to say the gentleman was embarrassed. Yet, the wonderful people turned it into a beautiful and unforgettable memory of two cultures, brought closer together. East is East. West is West. And, with understanding, the twain shall meet.

# CHAPTER THREE

# You Gotta Be Kidding

# One for the books

愛 愛 愛 愛 愛 愛 愛 愛 愛

*A* lovely family was staying at our Holiday Inn hotel while the builder put the finishing touches on their new home. Naturally, we had many chats, especially with the inquisitive 7 year-old son. We told him all about the Hotel business and all the different jobs we perform.

One rainy afternoon, the little boy came up to the Front Desk and very solemnly asked "Is the bookkeeper in, please?"

After telling him the bookkeeper was out, I asked what he wanted to see him about. The little fella exclaimed: "I'm bored and I just wanta know what kinda books he has to read!"

# Don't worry.
# The room will pay!

ða ða ða ða ða ða ða ða ða

*A* small child asked his mother for money to buy a soda. They were out by the pool and he was thirsty. The young mother told him, "I'm sorry, Son. I don't have any money. Why don't you go get a sip of water."

But, the little boy persisted. "I want a soda, not water!" he whined.

The young mother, who had exhausted her vacation budget, told him more firmly: "I don't have any more money." To which the little boy replied: "Well. Then charge it to the room. The Room will pay!"

# Lost and found

❧ ❧ ❧ ❧ ❧ ❧ ❧ ❧ ❧

*A*s the Executive Housekeeper at a Holiday Inn hotel in northern Texas, I received the following letter a few days after Christmas, obviously from a very young traveler.

Dear people,

I lost some toys, My white seal. Baby Mickey Mouse, walrus and Brown Bear. They got lost in Oklahoma. Go there to room 24 and get them. Bring them to me in San Antonio.

Sincerely,
Jared

P.S. A discreet phone call to the faraway Hotel led to the recovery of Jared's toys and we are happy to say they were sent to him in San Antonio (about 300 miles from our Hotel!).

# Buddy, can you spare a dime?

❧ ❧ ❧ ❧ ❧ ❧ ❧ ❧ ❧

*A*s the General Manager, I lived with my family in an apartment on the Hotel premises when a tornado struck our Holiday Inn hotel near Nashville. The storm severely damaged the roof in several areas.

While trying to get the Hotel back to normal, we set up buckets under the leaks.

One afternoon, one of our regular guests came up to me and said, "Well, Larry. I put in a donation for your new roof." I asked him was he meant and he explained that he had dropped some money into the "collection can."

Investigating, I soon came across the coffee can that my children had set up to collect donations for Muscular Dystrophy. Unable to spell the disease, they had simply labeled the can with a little sign: "Please help us. The Holiday Inn."

# The room fairies

❧ ❧ ❧ ❧ ❧ ❧ ❧ ❧ ❧

*M*y wife and I were traveling with our little girl. Each morning, we would get dressed and go out for breakfast. When we returned, the beds would be made and the carpet vacuumed.

On the third morning, as we were leaving our room, my little girl paused and asked, "Daddy, how do the room fairies know when we're gone so they can clean up our room?"

# I'd like room service, please

❧ ❧ ❧ ❧ ❧ ❧ ❧ ❧ ❧

*M*y young son was enchanted with Room Service. He thought it was just great to be able to pick up the phone, request a burger and fries whenever he felt hungry. After several days, he asked, "Why don't we get Room Service at home?"

His mother just groaned...

# Is that a dumb waiter or what?

🙙 🙙 🙙 🙙 🙙 🙙 🙙 🙙 🙙

One day a little girl and her mother came into the Dining Room for lunch. As I approached their table, the little girl asked about a coat, enclosed in glass, in the corner of the restaurant. After I explained that the coat had once belonged to Elvis and showed her the other mementos on display, her mother told me, half apologetically, that the little girl was very inquisitive and observant and that she never forgot anything.

I went on to describe the day's specials but, when I got to the soup of the day, I couldn't remember what it was. Trying to cover my blunder, I said "The soup has not been announced yet, so I will go to find out."

As I walked away, I heard the little girl ask "Mommy, do they have dumb waiters here?"

Determined to regain the child's respect, I delivered everything (and more) to perfection. As the meal progressed, the mother once again engaged me in conversation. She mentioned, again apologetically, her daughter's great thirst for knowledge.

She went on to say that, while they were staying in an old hotel in New York City, the little girl had seen these trays going up, some coming down and curious, had asked her mother what they were. Her mother told her they were dumb waiters and she thought all hotels had them.

Remembering her mother's comment that all hotels had dumb waiters, the little girl wanted to know if our Holiday Inn hotel had any...

Of course, I told her, "We have no dumb waiters here, ma'am!"

# The real world

೫ ೫ ೫ ೫ ೫ ೫ ೫ ೫ ೫

My 4-year old daughter and I were riding on a moving sidewalk at the newly constructed Holiday Inn hotel. Holding my hand, she looked up and said, "Wouldn't it be fun if they had this in the Real World!"

# CHAPTER FOUR

# Room at
the Inn

# A Christmas story

❧ ❧ ❧ ❧ ❧ ❧ ❧ ❧ ❧

*S*ome people make you proud to be a member of the human race. Rick is one of those people.

Rick is a shift leader at the Front Desk. One blustery November day, he was enjoying a day off, browsing through garage sales and thrift stores. At one stop, he caught bits of conversation between a lady and her little girl. The child was begging her mother to buy an old, dilapidated doll house for $15. The mother, struggling to maintain some dignity, reminded the little girl that they only had money for a coat. But the little girl kept begging. She promised she wouldn't even let herself feel the cold if she could only have the doll house. The mother's eyes welled with tears, but she hastily paid for the stained, rag tag coat and left.

Rick, totally on impulse, hopped into his car and discreetly followed them to a run-down house. He noted their address and quickly drove back to the thrift shop to buy the doll house.

He gathered paint and fabric and tools and proceeded to "renovate" the beat-up doll house. He even wallpapered the kitchen. Six weeks later, the doll house sparkled. It was now a colorful dream home, complete with miniature furnishings. Something even Santa could not improve upon.

In the cold, gray dawn of Christmas Day, Rick loaded his treasure into his car and drove over to the little girl's house. He gently cleared the snow from the front steps and carefully placed the doll house (wrapped only with a big red bow and letter from Santa) at the front door.

Not wanting to embarrass the family, he quietly drove away and spent the rest of his Christmas morning as Manager on Duty at the Hotel.

# The true spirit of Christmas

≈ ≈ ≈ ≈ ≈ ≈ ≈ ≈ ≈

December 1990 was another of my many Christmases spent on the road, away from my family and friends.

My home away from home, for the past three months, had been the Chattanooga Choo Choo Holiday Inn hotel. During this time, I ate most of my meals at the Hotel's Poolside Cafe and I became pretty well acquainted with most of the staff.

The Friday night before Christmas arrived and I was especially depressed and lonely. I worked late that night, trying to forget my troubles. Finally exhausted, I decided to go back to the Hotel.

As I opened the door to my room, I was delighted to find a fully-decorated Christmas tree centered on my coffee table. Bright lights and strands of gleaming tinsel twinkled at me. There was even a crockpot of warm clam chowder on the bar and a present under the tree. The card read, simply, "Your family at the Poolside Cafe."

Each year, as I spend the holidays with my family and friends, I remember that cold December night, when I discovered the true spirit of Christmas.

# A picnic in the rain

*Business* took one Priority Club member to the Holiday Inn hotel in Worcester, Massachusetts in mid-August. Being a Sunday, the drive, fly, drive routine did not allow much time to concentrate on the weather.

Monday morning, he awoke to rain. Nothing unusual in New England. After his morning coffee, he proceeded to the days work and was met by his contact with what could only be described as incredulity. He explained that a major hurricane was tracking towards Boston and at 12:00 noon a state of emergency would go into effect. All vehicles had to be off the roadways. The plant would close to allow all personnel to get home by noon. They agreed to begin work, if possible, the next day and the man drove back to the Hotel.

He went up to his room and opened the curtain to watch the storm. He turned on the weather channel and began to catch up on paperwork. Throughout the next several hours he watched the storm move up the Eastern seaboard on the television. He also observed, while looking out the window at the storm, that the parking lot was beginning to fill.

About 4:30 p.m., he decided to go down and have an early dinner, before the restaurant got crowded.

Upon arriving in the lobby, he was greeted by a mob scene. It seems the reason the parking lot was filling up was a result of the state of emergency. Also, since all the local restaurant and fast food outlets were closed, this was the only game in town. Asking the Hostess how long he would have to wait, he was shocked when she replied, "6 to 8 hours...if we don't run out of food."

He stood there, not knowing what to do. The waiter who had served him dinner the night before (when there were only two people in the Dining Room) recognized him and asked if he could help. The man explained his situation and suggested that any help in getting served would be most appreciated. The waiter smiled and disappeared into the crowd. A few minutes later, he returned with a paper bag. Inside was a sandwich and chips — it seemed a gourmet feast!

# *Holly Lynn*

#### ❧ ❧ ❧ ❧ ❧ ❧ ❧ ❧ ❧

*I*t was a very cold and windy evening in late November, 1989. The Hotel was quiet, only a few rooms were rented. The banquet complex was full. The bar was hopping and the Dining Room was packed. The sleeping rooms were few, so not many guests were roaming the halls.

One of our guests was disturbed in his room. He heard a baby crying. He left his room and spotted a box. When he looked in it, he saw a baby!

He immediately started running to the Front Desk, screaming, "Come quick! There's a baby in a box! Quick! Come!"

The Assistant Manager quickly followed the guest down the corridor and there, in the box, was a tiny newborn baby. He picked the box up and ran! The General Manager immediately took charge. Holding the baby under her jacket, next to her body to try to keep her warm, Bev instructed her staff. Police and an ambulance were dispatched. There was no time to waste. The tiny newborn was critical, suffering from hypothermia and blood loss. The doctors worked desperately into the night trying to save her tiny life. At last our baby was stabilized.

Two police officers, a detective and our General Manager conducted a room to room search, but they found nothing. The search, the questions, the evening became long and confusing. What could have happened? As the hours passed, it became obvious that the mother had delivered somewhere else and then abandoned the baby at our Hotel. The media went crazy!

The next day, the newspapers were telling our story...The Hotel guests, the employees and the locals brought gifts, clothing and money for the Holiday Inn hotel's youngest unregistered guest— newly named Holly Lynn.

Adoptive parents brought Holly Lynn home from the hospital, just in time for Christmas and we all rejoiced that this special little girl had found a loving home.

To this day, the parents bring Holly Lynn and her charming brothers to visit.

# CHAPTER FIVE

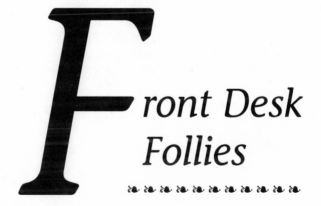

ront Desk
Follies

# Have you two met?

za za za za za za za za

One evening, a nearby Hotel called to inquire if we could accommodate an angry, overbooked, late arrival. I took the reservation and alerted the bellman that a Mr. "Smith" would be arriving in the competitor's limo and that we might capture his future business if we were extremely attentive.

Minutes later, I registered Mr. John Smith, an obviously tired, perturbed traveler. I presented him a complimentary cocktail card and a most cordial welcome.

Since it was a busy evening in our Dining Room, I also asked Mr. Smith if I might reserve a table for him. He was most appreciative and asked for time to settle in prior to eating. He headed for his room and I called the restaurant.

Unbeknownst to me, a *Dr.* John Smith had checked in earlier that day. At 8:20 p.m., he phoned the Dining Room to cancel his table, opting for Room Service. He then ordered a full dinner, to be delivered while he stepped out for a minute.

The plot thickens.

At 8:30 p.m., *Mr.* Smith entered a fully-booked Dining Room, only to learn that his table had been canceled — as per his request! In spite of his protests, he would simply have to wait. Seeing the blood rush to his face, the Hostess offered complimentary cocktails in the adjacent lounge. The hungry, tired, stymied Mr. Smith acquiesced.

At 8:45, *Dr.* Smith left his room to visit the gift shop, browsing through the magazines and books. Meanwhile, *Mr.* Smith, finishing a second martini, glanced at his watch and decided to go up and order Room Service.

Around 9:00 pm, *Dr.* Smith purchased a novel and walked toward the elevator. As *Mr.* Smith walked past the Front Desk, I called him over to give him a telephone message. Assuming he'd just finished dinner, I asked if everything was to his satisfaction. He stopped in his tracks, sneered at me and mumbled something about Room Service.

Entering his room, *Mr.* Smith was delighted by the sight of a lovely table, set with a three course dinner, wine, coffee and fresh flowers. He decided to go right down to the Front Desk to thank me and apologize for his recent behavior.

Of course, *Dr.* Smith was concerned when he returned to his room and found no dinner there to greet him. He phoned Room Service, but the call was intercepted by the Dining Room Hostess, gushing about having a table available, but not having been able to locate him in the lounge.

Hollywood could not have scripted a better scene.

A distinguished, older gentleman urgently approached me at the Front Desk. Suddenly, Mr. Smith, whom I recognized, comes up with equal determination. I asked the first man his name. He replies, "Dr. John Smith."

With that, Mr. John Smith bursts into laughter, turns, and offers his hand. After a quick, hysterical recounting of the evening's events, we soon had the two Smiths comfortably seated — together — in our Dining Room, enjoying two much-deserved dinners on the house.

# Executive V.P.
## of rubber duckies

🦆 🦆 🦆 🦆 🦆 🦆 🦆 🦆 🦆

*O*ur indoor Holidome recreation facility has been a major attraction from the day it opened. The hot tub is especially popular during our cold Midwestern winter months.

One chilly day, a rather pompous, burly guest came up to the Front Desk, clad only in dripping bathing shorts. He reported the hot tub out of order and demanded that it be repaired at once. The guest was asked to return to the hot tub with the promise that the Front Desk Clerk would immediately follow to determine the problem.

As the clerk rushed into the Holidome, his eye was drawn to the kiddie pool, occupied solely by this guest.

"Oh, my!" thought the clerk. "There's the problem...he thinks he's in the hot tub!" Which presented another problem. How to get him out of there without embarrassment?

The quick-witted clerk politely informed the guest that, indeed, this tub was not functioning, but that another one was located at the other end of the swimming pool and in perfect order.

The guest trotted down to the "other" hot tub — happily ignorant of his gaff — and the clerk went on to solve other major crises.

# Make that a single, please

❧ ❧ ❧ ❧ ❧ ❧ ❧ ❧ ❧

*B*ecause of a big softball tournament one weekend, all the Hotels in town were booked solid, including the Holiday Inn hotel. With a lobby full of people begging for rooms, we welcomed any cancellations we could get.

No matter where we got them.

And a cancellation came in early that Friday afternoon: "I'd like to cancel a reservation, please" the female caller explained. "Our plans have changed."

All was well and good until later that evening when the rush of check-ins arrived. As one couple approached the Front Desk, the gentleman said he had reservations and stated his name. I called the name up on my computer screen and immediately informed him: "I am so sorry, sir. We gave your room to someone else. Your reservation was canceled this morning."

"What?!" he yelled. "Canceled? By Whom?"

"Your wife, sir." I replied.

With that, the guest — and his attractive female companion — meekly walked away.

# You must be jockeying

*ta ta ta ta ta ta ta ta ta*

$O$ur Hotel had a block of rooms set aside for
people coming into town for the annual horse
show. I was working the third shift by myself when
one of the jockeys walked up to the Front Desk.
Bare-chested, he looked down at himself and
asked, "Could you help me get out of these?"

Now I've been asked to perform many tasks,
but none so shocking as this. My surprised look led
him to further explain: "It's really hard to do without help and my buddy is still at the track," he
implored.

"You can't take your pants off by yourself?" I
asked, incredulously.

"Oh! No!" he laughed, backing away from the
desk. Pointing to his feet, he said, "I'm talking
about my riding boots!"

# *A little attention is all we ask*

&a &a &a &a &a &a &a &a &a

One winter, our area was hit by a series of severe ice and snow storms. On several occasions, our Holiday Inn hotel was called upon to house stranded crowds, turning our banquet rooms into makeshift dormitories. Truckers would sleep six to a room. People even slept on the floor. It seemed the worst winter since the Ice Age.

One afternoon, the highway department started closing down the highways once again and people began to pour into the lobby. For what seemed to be hours, confusion reigned at the Front Desk, with people clamoring for the few beds we had left. A few children in the crowd kept jumping up and down, adding to the melee.

Suddenly, I heard some tiny voices shout in unison: "DO YOU HAVE *ANY* ROOMS LEFT???"

The entire crowd froze and turned in unison. There, in the center of the lobby, were four "little people" with their hands cupped to amplify their voices. They weren't children after all, but adults who were being rudely upstaged by a rather insensitive, tired crowd.

I checked them into the last room we had — a single.

And, they didn't mind one bit. They said they could all sleep very comfortably with that much room.

# Time is money

❧ ❧ ❧ ❧ ❧ ❧ ❧ ❧ ❧

*O*nce a month, a traveling salesman, driving a big, old station wagon loaded with books, papers, magazines and luggage, pulls up in front of our Hotel.

This little man, with gray hair, gets out of his car like a tornado, ready to hit. He runs to the Front Desk and expects to be waited on right away. He doesn't care who is there, saying "Time is Money. Hurry! Hurry!" I do my best to get him settled fast so he can get comfortable.

His next step is to get everything out of his car. And, I do mean everything! He never wants any help. After an hour or two, he orders Room Service and a few drinks. He calls the Front Desk for more wash cloths. He likes several when he takes a shower. He says this is an another luxury of staying at the Holiday Inn hotel.

He gets started cutting out his pictures and articles from all his books and magazines. He sometimes stays two nights and when he leaves, he leaves millions of pieces of paper on the floor.

He once told me that he lived alone and if he had to clean up after himself, it would cut into his time and money. That's why he comes to the Holiday Inn hotel! We are a family Hotel and he considers us his family!

# May I show you your room?

*T*he grand opening of our beautiful new Hotel was exciting for all of us. Our eager new Guest Services Representative anxiously awaited her first customer.

A man walked in and approached the Front Desk. No sooner did our Guest Services Representative ask if she could help him, than his eyes rolled back and he collapsed to the floor. Unconscious. An ambulance was called and, as he was being wheeled out, the overzealous Guest Services Representative chased after him.

She leaned into the stretcher and, with new job eagerness, asked the lifeless guest if he'd like to guarantee a room for his return visit.

(Of course, the medics recognized her condition for what it was — shock. And the poor Guest Services Representative got to go for an ambulance ride, too.)

# Would you prefer
# a silent alarm?

❧ ❧ ❧ ❧ ❧ ❧ ❧ ❧ ❧

One cranky guest demanded a free room because the fire alarm had jarred him from a sound sleep.

When politely asked if he would prefer not to hear the alarm at all, he quietly, humbly rescinded his request for complimentary accommodations.

# I've got to go

≈ ≈ ≈ ≈ ≈ ≈ ≈ ≈ ≈

*A* distinguished guest approached the Front Desk and asked how to get to the restroom. The Guest Services Representative on duty gave him discreet directions.

Minutes later, the guest reappeared, looking bewildered. "Ma'am, I must've taken a wrong turn. I just couldn't seem to find the restroom. Where did you say it is, again?"

The Guest Services Representative repeated her directions. "It's the door right behind you and to the left, sir."

He thanked her and left. Only to come back again, more anxious than ever. And, no wonder.

"Look, Miss. I've got a real problem. I'm the guest speaker at a meeting being held in your West Room. And I am late. PLEASE, show me where the West Room is."

The mystery was solved. We have no West Room. His meeting was in the East Room, not the rest room!

# Check up on check out

&a &a &a &a &a &a &a &a &a

*O*ne evening, a guest approached the Front Desk and asked "What time is check out?"

I replied "1:00 p.m., sir."

The guest, a young man obviously new to traveling, thanked me and slowly walked away. I watched the frowning young man pace up and down the lobby for a few minutes. He finally returned to the Front Desk with an anguished expression on his face and asked, "Would it be possible to check out before one o'clock? I can't stay here till then; I've got to meet someone at ten."

# You never know
# unless you ask

ðŸ¦† ðŸ¦† ðŸ¦† ðŸ¦† ðŸ¦† ðŸ¦† ðŸ¦† ðŸ¦† ðŸ¦†

*A* production company was filming a movie near our Hotel. Weeks before the crew's arrival, the company placed an ad in our local newspaper. People interested in being "extras" could apply at our Hotel, the nearby Holiday Inn hotel.

One of our Front Desk clerks, excited by the announcement, was eager to apply. She told many of her coworkers that she especially wanted to play the part of a saucy Western dance hall girl.

Well, the crew finally arrived to begin production. Early Friday morning, one of our longtime guests walked up to the Front Desk. He and the clerk were engaged in polite conversation when she blurted out, "I'd love to be a prostitute. Do you need one?"

The guest turned purple and my mouth dropped open as I realized the reason for her faux pas. The guest looked very much like the producer, who was just then walking towards the desk.

I explained the situation and our guest was truly charming about it. In fact, as he turned to leave, he said to the beautiful young clerk, "By the way, in answer to your question...YES!"

# CHAPTER SIX

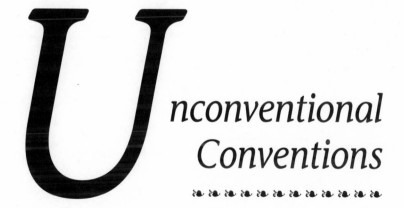

# U nconventional Conventions

# Traveling has its ups and downs

❧ ❧ ❧ ❧ ❧ ❧ ❧ ❧

*D*uring an incredibly busy convention season, it was brought to the attention of management that we had a very disgruntled conventioneer on our hands.

His complaint to the Front Desk was "Your hotel obviously lacks the proper security. For most of the night, the door to my room was repeatedly opened and closed, opened and closed. With people coming in and out, all night long. I could hardly sleep at all!"

Needless to say, the management was very concerned...Until further investigation, that is.

It seems the fellow had had so much fun the night before in the Hospitality Suite that he'd fallen asleep in the elevator. Where he'd spent much of the night. Before he woke up in the morning, his pals had discovered him and deposited him safely in his own room, where he awoke with a headache and vague memories of people entering and leaving his "room!"

# Triple treat

*I*t was the first weekend in January in the heart of quiet, quaint New England. What a memorable weekend was in store for us all!

Earlier in the week, "Mr. Smith" came to talk with our General Manager about booking a gathering. He was president of a club dedicated to allowing men the freedom to express their feminine side. Once they arrived, his group would dress as women and he asked that the entire staff address them as women. He concluded by saying: "By the way, you won't recognize me after today. You'll know me as Betty Lee."

This alone would have been enough to spice up our week. But, wait. There's more.

We also had a conservative religious group coming in.

Plus, the LaLeche League (which promotes breast feeding until the child loses interest).

The potential for confrontation was definite. And, the upcoming winter freeze almost guaranteed that all attendees would stay within the warm comfort of the Hotel.

Yes, it was just a matter of time...

Early into the weekend, a "club" member came to the front office with a complaint. He/she was appalled to encounter a woman breast feeding her son, right by the indoor pool. The Manager gave him/her a smiling "once-over" glance and the guest replied, "I see what you mean" and went off to the group's fashion show.

The ladies' restroom was another challenge.

The religious group, renowned for speaking their beliefs to anyone they meet, for some reason felt no calling to recruit the "club" members. They did, however, object to the members using the ladies' restroom.

The LaLeche women, in turn, called to complain about the "club" members parading around the pool in full make up and two-piece bathing suits.

Our skills of diplomacy and tact were put to the test. Each crisis brought a new solution and by the end of the weekend, we had three distinctly different groups cheerfully interacting with one another.

# *Every witch way*

‌&‌ ‌&‌ ‌&‌ ‌&‌ ‌&‌ ‌&‌ ‌&‌ ‌&‌ ‌&‌

*D*uring the Fall of 1990, our Holiday Inn hotel was the headquarters hotel for the Southwestern Division of Witches Convention.

The ballroom was filled with display tables of fascinating magical paraphernalia. Every day, we would take discreet, curious peeks at the oddities on display: crystal balls, buzzard toes, frog tongues, Ouija boards and such.

But the magic wasn't just on the tables.

When the witches were in the restaurant, experienced busboys dropped trays and dishes seemed to fly from waiters' hands. As these special guests passed the Front Desk, computers went down and the Holidex reservation system malfunctioned.

On the last day of the Convention — needless to say, we were primed to expect anything — we heard SLAM! SLAM! SLAM!

All of the doors on the first floor suddenly slammed shut. For no reason. There was no fire alarm. Nothing to prompt such action.

At least, nothing you could see or touch.

# R 'n R = C 'n W.  and
# that's A-O.K.

❧ ❧ ❧ ❧ ❧ ❧ ❧ ❧ ❧

*D*uring the summer of 1987, a hot Rock 'n Roll band was scheduled to play a concert in Vail and stayed at our Hotel.

The night before the concert, the band's manager noted that our Lounge was having a quiet night and he offered a special treat to our employees, if we closed early.

Well, word spread quickly among the staff, both those on duty and those at home. We gathered with great excitement and at midnight, the rocker and his buddies appeared. But, in place of the expected 200-decibel amplifiers and such, they were carrying acoustic guitars.

In a gentle tone, the rocker explained, "It's hard to relax when you're on the road so much. But, we've enjoyed this place so much, we wanted to show you how we unwind."

For the next hour, this master of boogie, blues and rock played the sweetest Country 'n Western music you've ever heard — a far cry from the frenzied sold-out performance the next night.

# The Snowlympics

❧ ❧ ❧ ❧ ❧ ❧ ❧ ❧ ❧

$\mathcal{A}$s GM of a Holiday Inn hotel in North Platte, Nebraska, I have seen my share of snowstorms. But nothing like the blizzard of March 28, 1980.

It was the kind of storm you simply had to wait out. And, as the local interstate roads closed, and one weary traveler after another straggled in, I realized we wouldn't be waiting it out alone. Pretty soon, our Hotel was filled to capacity and we were even making preparations for an additional 700 guests in our Holidome.

The situation could have been unbearable were it not for the generous donation of cases of soft drinks from the local Coca-Cola bottler and a group of truckers waiting out the storm.

Using Cokes as prizes, the drivers organized a makeshift winter Olympics to keep the stranded children occupied.

There were snowman building competitions, swimming contests, and even talent shows.

When the interstates finally reopened three days later, everyone agreed that what began as a natural disaster ended up a winter wonderland.

# Lady's luck

☙ ☙ ☙ ☙ ☙ ☙ ☙ ☙ ☙

*B*ecause our Hotel is located near a large casino in the upper Midwest, we get many bus tours and groups of people with the gambling bug. But, no one would have figured the odds of a bus from Chicago and another from Detroit bringing good fortune like this...

Normally, tour buses arrive on a staggered schedule to allow time to check in one busload of guests before the next group arrives. Normally, that is.

Two buses pulled in at the same time one hot summer day, filled with tired guests who were eager to shower and get to the gaming tables. The luggage was piled up en masse in the parking lot and the buses departed. The staff set out to quickly sort it all and hand deliver it to each room

About 20 minutes into this ordeal, a woman from Chicago came to the Front Desk to ask if she could help, in hopes of finding her own bag. We relented and put her in charge of distributing some luggage to the second floor. She knocked on the first door and waited. When the door opened, she screamed.

And so did the woman at the door.

The two were sisters who hadn't seen each other for six years. And, being avid gamblers, they saw this good luck as an omen and giddily rushed to the casino. Hand in hand.

Looked to me like they already hit the jackpot!

# Culture clash

ᴥ ᴥ ᴥ ᴥ ᴥ ᴥ ᴥ ᴥ ᴥ

*W*e were host to two weddings. A total of 480 people would be dining with us that evening. One group was a gracious wedding party of 280 and the other was comprised of 200 motorcycle riders (each of whom had brought his bike for display).

As the evening wound down and the parties came to a close, people began to filter out. I was called to the Front Desk. A gentleman had discovered that his car was blocked by one of the motorcycles. I asked him to wait for a moment as I was certain I could find someone who would recognize the bike and move it for him.

I located the groom of the biker wedding (a rather large man) and asked him to come with me to identify the bike. As we walked outside, we witnessed three considerably smaller gentlemen picking up the bike to move it out of the way.

My heart raced and my vision blurred. If anyone knows anything at all about motorcycles, he knows the one thing you do not do is move or touch them. I could just see an all out war between the weddings!

The biker groom was gracious enough to turn the other way as I convinced the three men to put the bike down. Gently.

The groom said to me "You're lucky it's my wedding day. Tomorrow I won't remember what just happened. And, I won't tell my friend 'Killer' what they just did to his bike!"

# Now that I have your attention...

&#x279c; &#x279c; &#x279c; &#x279c; &#x279c; &#x279c; &#x279c; &#x279c; &#x279c;

*F*or many years, I have held a General Manager's reception for our guests every Monday evening. Near the end of the reception we have a drawing for door prizes.

I announce the door prize drawing by saying, "LAST WEEK we gave away a Mercedes and a trip around the world." After I have everyone's attention (which I now definitely have), I say "And, this week we are giving away a cookbook and a road atlas!"

This final announcement is always well-received, in the spirit intended.

Also, the cookbook and road atlas are in the operating budget!

# A party with a new twist

ᨠ ᨠ ᨠ ᨠ ᨠ ᨠ ᨠ ᨠ ᨠ

*I*t was springtime in Appleton, Wisconsin and the Holiday Inn hotel was host to a seminar to help smokers quit the habit. All 229 rooms were booked and all of our guests were, obviously, already on edge.

Worrying about a tornado was not on their agenda.

When word came over our weather transmitter that we were under a "watch," which was quickly upgraded to a "warning," their nerves grew even more frazzled.

Fortunately, within our midst was a very sociable musician — a jovial tuba player who was booked to perform with a Dixieland band that night.

He hit upon a great idea. Escorting the entire lounge full of guests down to the safety of our basement, he lead them with the festive sound of his tuba. We offered complimentary refreshments to wait out the storm.

After the "all-clear" was sounded, the now-slightly tipsy guests wobbled out of the basement and back up to their rooms. One participant passed the Front Desk, then leaned back and said, in a slurred fashion, "That was the best tornado party I've ever been to. Can we do it again?"

# CHAPTER SEVEN

omantics and
Other Antics

# Save your breath

⋙ ⋙ ⋙ ⋙ ⋙ ⋙ ⋙ ⋙ ⋙

*F*resh from Desert Storm service in Saudi Arabia, a group of air crew members were greatly enjoying our swimming pool and beer. Having been so long denied either pleasure, one beer led to another. And another.

It was great to see "our boys" home and enjoying themselves after the recent tedium in the Gulf. Their fun seemed harmless enough until we got a frantic call from a female guest: "Quick! I think they're going to kill a naked lady!"

The Manager on Duty rushed to the pool and was alarmed to see two crewmen on a balcony, poised to toss what appeared to be a naked woman over the railing, down to their buddies in the pool. A second look, however, revealed the "lady" to be a life-sized inflatable doll.

The Manager on Duty cracked up, but it took almost 30 minutes to calm the lady who'd reported the "impending violence."

He finally escorted the distraught woman to the restaurant. Where he was both shocked and relieved when she burst out laughing. Following her gaze, he witnessed the formal entrance of the air crew — escorting the properly dressed doll to dinner!

# You light up my wife

ð ð ð ð ð ð ð ð ð

*A*n out-of-town organization decided on our Hotel as the site of their first annual Marriage Enrichment Retreat. The couples arrived and everything was going smoothly — until the power went out.

An electric company official told us that a car had hit a power pole and we could expect to endure at least five hours without electricity. Immediately, the staff tried to make the best of a bad situation.

Porters went to purchase extra flashlights, batteries and candles. The kitchen pulled out generators, sterno and gas grills. In general, the Hotel was a beehive of activity to save the day...and night.

Our Enrichment Retreat guests had been alerted to the situation and were surprised to hear that dinner would begin as scheduled. In fact, they were told that the Manager would throw in a "romantic, candlelight dinner" with our compliments!

From that point on, everyone made "light" of the situation and the Enrichment group enhanced their agenda with fun and romance. Aglow over their dinner, they gathered in the lobby before retiring. They ribbed us about planning the outage for their "enlightenment." Not missing a beat, we

had a brilliant idea: we told them that we'd ar-
ranged to take their phones off the hook (the
switchboard being inoperative) so that they
wouldn't be disturbed.

Escorting couples to their rooms, we had the
porter claim that we had special-ordered candles,
made from magical "romance" wax.

"No one asked for extra blankets!" shouted
someone, as the group adjourned to their rooms.

One husband complained that he would be
unable to watch the Piston's Playoff Game. "We'll
have a playoff of our own," promised his wife.

Shortly after 10 p.m., the power returned. The
next morning, our apologies were met with, "Non-
sense! The power failure was the brightest part of
our weekend!"

The Marriage Enrichment Retreat has returned
to our Holiday Inn hotel every year since then —
with complimentary candlelight always included!

# A very bad connection

ta ta ta ta ta ta ta ta ta

*M*y first night as a Front Desk Clerk years ago is one for the book!

Switchboard technology has come a long way since the night I was manning a rather old-fashioned switchboard which required that I manually switch phone lines, matching cords to corresponding flashing lights.

After three hours, I thought I had mastered my job. A woman called, asking to speak with her husband — a truck driver who had checked in that evening.

The sheer volume of calls, coupled with my overconfidence, made for the blunder of the day: I connected the woman with her husband...

As he was talking with his girlfriend on another line!

Talk about static on the line!!

# *My little chickadee*

*A*s the Food & Beverage Director at a beachside
Holiday Inn hotel in Florida, I presided over the
lounge. Our most popular drinks were called
"Hisacane and Heracane" - concoctions which
played an important part in one of the biggest
moments in honeymoon history.

Alerted by the Front Desk to be on the look-
out for a honeymoon couple who had reservations
for dinner and dancing, I was intrigued, upon their
arrival, by their sheer physical proportion.

The gentleman appeared to weigh well over
300 pounds and his lovely bride was in the same
range. They took their seats and, when not on the
dance floor, partook of an unusual quantity of
"acanes." Soon, a full case of the keepsake glasses
was stacked under their table.

And not long after, their waitress tapped me
on the shoulder. The new husband had requested
my assistance.

Going to their table, I found the bride passed
out cold. Her husband asked for my help in trans-
porting his beloved to their room. There being no
way I could carry, drag, lug or otherwise move the
bride, I sent for a busboy and a luggage cart from
the lobby. Together, with the help of the stout
groom and a dishwasher, we loaded the bride, her

purse, and the case of empty souvenir glasses onto the cart.

Reaching the wedding chamber, we placed the inert bride on the left side of the bed, contentedly snoring away.

As I bade the young man a good night, he shook my hand, thanking me for the most exciting night of his life!

# *Where did you two meet?*

🦆 🦆 🦆 🦆 🦆 🦆 🦆 🦆 🦆

*I*n January, 1986, I was transferred as a petroleum landman from Texas to Michigan, where the oil and gas business was relatively active. I checked into the Holiday Inn hotel on that cold January day with only one thing on my mind...work! However, being a young man of 26, it was difficult not to notice the young ladies at the Front Desk, especially the cute ones.

One day, while requesting information at the Front Desk, I was told that I should come back the following day after 3:00 p.m. The comment was followed up (every so slyly) by a young man telling me to come back when "Denise" was working. I tried to act like I did not hear the remark, however, it was difficult because the young lady standing next to the guy punched him, indicating he'd let the cat out of the bag.

By the next day, I'd nearly forgotten the incident when I was cashing a check at the Front Desk. All of a sudden, it hit me. I looked at the name tag of the young lady helping me...and KaBam! It was Denise. My heart rate instantly soared. She was definitely one of the cute ones.

From that time on, the tactics used by her co-workers to get us together were quite humorous.

For instance, one morning I was in my room working. Denise was at home, getting ready for her afternoon shift. My phone rang and at that very moment, so did hers (unknown to me). Well, we both answered. "Hello?" After a few anxious seconds, we began talking. Each assumed the other had called. Not until she arrived for work did her coworkers spill the beans. A fellow desk clerk had mischievously connected Denise's outside line with my room line. As a direct result of this fiasco, we enjoyed our first date and on May 9, 1987, we married. Much of our first year of marriage was spent in Room 247 of the Holiday Inn hotel.

Well, it's been almost five years now and we never fail to get a laugh or two when we are asked "How did you two meet?"

# Strangers in the night

æ æ æ æ æ æ æ æ æ

Although we work for different companies, my wife and I always stay at Holiday Inn hotels during our frequent travels around the country.

While on a week long trip, I decided to stay at the Hotel in a small town for a meeting with several of my sales reps — and to watch a hockey game on TV.

The game was exciting — so much so that, at times, we got pretty loud. So loud, in fact, that the person in the adjoining room called the Hotel's management several times to complain. Soon, our little party was forced to break up.

As I settled into bed and turned off the TV, I heard the set next door blaring away. Deciding to "return the favor," I called the Front Desk to complain. In a few minutes, the other set was turned off and I settled back with a satisfied smile.

A few days later, over Saturday morning coffee, my wife and I were exchanging accounts of the previous week's travels. She said the most annoying event of her week was a loud party in the room next to her in a Holiday Inn hotel where she'd stopped for an unplanned stayover — going on to say that she had to call the desk several times to complain and that the rude person had the nerve to call the desk about HER TV!

Unlike the night of the game, I kept my mouth shut.

# Reach out and tease someone

❧ ❧ ❧ ❧ ❧ ❧ ❧ ❧ ❧

*L*ast Fall, a nice elderly couple stayed at our Hotel for several days. As they were checking out, the clerk noticed a long distance telephone charge on their bill in the amount of $1,824.02.

The clerk grimaced at the obvious error and, chuckling, showed it to the husband before adjusting it off the bill. The man asked that he wait for just a minute. He wanted to play a joke on his wife.

He called his wife over and angrily waved the bill. "Look at the size of this phone bill," he said. "Just try to convince ME you don't talk too much!"

Luckily, she had a sense of humor to match.

# True confession

ぁ ぁ ぁ ぁ ぁ ぁ ぁ ぁ ぁ

*H*ow do you tell your husband that he almost missed the wedding??

Each year the local Holiday Inn hotel hosts a Christmas party to honor our customers and friends. Each year, my staff and I go over the guest list and, as General Manager, I always greet each invitee.

While exchanging a handshake with most guests, some longtime male friends give me a hug or peck on the cheek. But one year, a local dentist came through the door and kissed me right on the lips!

Who, I wondered, is this man? My assistant reminded me that he was on our guest list and, because I didn't recognize his name, I had planned to strike him from the list. My staff convinced me to leave him on for one more year...

So, there we were. He returned for another kiss and a hug. Later still, he found a way to ask if I were married or engaged. When I replied in the negative, he asked me to dinner — and I accepted.

Five months later, we were married.

Eight years later, he's still on the list!

# *What goes up...*

&a &a &a &a &a &a &a &a &a

$A$ client scheduled her husband's big 40th birthday party at our Holiday Inn hotel. An accountant, she was very organized, attending to each small detail, anxious that everything be just right.

On the big night, all was going smoothly, just as planned.

Except for the most spectacular moment of the entire evening: the "Balloon Drop." The idea was for hundreds of balloons to be released from their netting and drift down upon the guests.

When the balloons were released, instead of descending over the merrymakers, they stayed "glued" to the ceiling — which is what helium-filled balloons almost always do!

# CHAPTER EIGHT

# Front Desk? There's a Bear in My Bed!

❧ ❧ ❧ ❧ ❧ ❧ ❧ ❧ ❧ ❧

# *A hotel can be a circus*

One scorchingly hot August day in 1989, people flocked to town for the Annual Frontier Days Festival and the Hotel staff scurried to accommodate our guests.

Around midnight, a terrific thunder storm brewed on the horizon. It grew to tumultuous proportions, offering up an alarming electrical storm. This, in turn, drove an unannounced guest to seek shelter inside our building.

As the night auditor was finalizing her reports, a shriek echoed through the lobby. Close behind our breathless Housekeeper, was a large brown bear. The latter, curious about his new surroundings, rushed to the Front Desk, his paw scraping across the counter, projecting the desk calendar across the room.

A call to the kitchen brought the morning cook, donut in hand, to lure our visitor away. But, the bear's taste ran more to greens. He loped over to a large plant by the sofa — and sat down to graze comfortably.

Our terror was growing, needless to say. Our frantic call to the police station brought officers poste-haste — who then decided to order back up forces.

Meanwhile, the bear wanted an after-dinner swim and headed for the Holidome, with the police in hot pursuit. But, the bear thought it was a game and alternated dips in the pool with scary lunges toward his new opponents.

Suddenly one of the desk clerks remembered a guest's comment about needing to house a large animal for the next day's parade. On the off chance this was the animal, she called the room. In seconds, the bear's owner appeared, clad in boxer shorts and a tee-shirt.

Everyone watched as he tackled the big, brown bear and brought him under control, earning a big, early-morning round of applause!

# I'm an animal till I have my morning coffee

☙ ☙ ☙ ☙ ☙ ☙ ☙ ☙ ☙

*E*arly one morning I began fielding frantic telephone calls from guests claiming the presence of a leopard — yes, a leopard — on property.

People reported seeing a man walking the animal on a leash, but, we had no idea where to look for this man and his leopard. Until, that is, a call came in to Room Service.

The order for Room 108 started out as a typical breakfast: two eggs, bacon, grits, toast, black coffee...

And, two raw chickens!

I didn't take the time to ask if he was ordering for the alleged unwelcome visitor. With police assistance, we simply restored the guest roster to human proportions.

# Everything was just ducky

🐤 🐤 🐤 🐤 🐤 🐤 🐤 🐤 🐤

*O*ur Holiday Inn hotel has a small canal running along the back of the property. This canal is home to turtles, ducks, and other wildlife.

One chilly, Spring afternoon, a regular guest rushed up to the Front Desk, calling for help. He had observed a mallard duck and her ducklings attempting to climb out of the pond. But they seemed too tired to stay afloat.

We all rushed to the bank where the guest was already frantically scooping up the ducklings with his hands, while the mother duck flapped her wings in confusion.

There were eleven fragile ducklings in all, some so weak, it looked like they were not going to make it. We finished scooping them up and brought them inside. After a gentle, soothing blow dry, the ducklings looked better. We finally located a woman who rehabilitates wild fowl and turned them over to her able charge.

One week later, all but one duckling had survived and we were delighted to learn that the survivors would be released into the wild.

# Going ape

❦ ❦ ❦ ❦ ❦ ❦ ❦ ❦ ❦

$S$uddenly, on a quiet and perfectly normal day, our Front Desk was swamped with frantic calls from alarmed guests...

A honeymoon couple claimed that eyes were staring at them.

A businessman said someone was trying to break in and steal something.

An elderly woman said there were ghosts in her room.

And children ran through the building shouting, "Gremlins!"

Finally, one call solved the mystery. It seems a guest had smuggled his monkey into his room in a covered cage, concealing its presence from the Front Desk. While he laid down for a nap, the animal got out of the cage and pried loose the grate over the air conditioning duct. This was before our renovation, so the ductwork ran in a straight line, past all the rooms.

The monkey had run through the ducts, peering into room after room. As guests reacted in horror, the monkey panicked and the chaos grew. If his owner had not called in search of his lost pet, I'm afraid I may have suspected "gremlins" myself!

# The old shell game

☙ ☙ ☙ ☙ ☙ ☙ ☙ ☙ ☙

*W*hen a guest at our beachfront Hotel called to complain about a mouse in the room, I promptly sent a bellman to move the family to another room — with our profuse apologies — even though I did not think it was probable that we had mice anywhere in the Hotel.

But, when they called with the same complaint from the second room, I went personally to escort them to a third room.

As I was helping them gather their things, the lady said, "There it goes again! Behind my purse!"

I saw a pile of seashells on the dresser — a common sight at a beachfront Hotel — next to her purse. And sure enough, there was a small intruder. But, it wasn't a mouse.

Careful inspection revealed it to be a harmless hermit crab, skittering from shell to shell. I returned it to the sea and the family returned to their vacation, uninterrupted by "unwelcome guests."

# Dog gone sight

☙ ☙ ☙ ☙ ☙ ☙ ☙ ☙ ☙

$\mathcal{M}$ost Hotels tend to frown on having dogs as overnight guests, but our Holiday Inn hotel has gained a reputation as an excellent venue for dog shows, so we get our share of canine guests. Most of them seem to be quite satisfied.

But not all.

One sunny afternoon, I was sitting with the General Manager in her office, talking. As I was admiring the view out her window, I caught the strangest sight — a German Shepherd in free-fall!

We rushed around to the side of the building and sure enough, there was a large Shepherd puppy, who had climbed onto a balcony table and slipped off.

Luckily, the animal wasn't injured. As we were recovering from the shock, a wise-cracking desk clerk rushed in with a scrawled note, claiming it was found in a third-story room.

"Arf, arf, arf, arf!" he read aloud.

"It seems clear enough to me," said the clerk, "that you guys just witnessed an attempted suicide."

He was barking up the wrong tree, of course.

# The cat caper

❧ ❧ ❧ ❧ ❧ ❧ ❧ ❧ ❧

*W*hen the Los Angeles Convention Center was host to a cat show across the street, our rooms were filled to capacity with cat owners and thousands of dollars worth of championship cats.

About 1 p.m. one afternoon, a cat owner came to the Front Desk, completely distraught. He and his wife could not find their prize cat.

Quickly, I organized a search party of staff and show attendees and we soon located the missing cat — inside the wall of a guest room! The animal was near the air conditioner, so we began to remove the unit so that we could rescue him. But, the cat, in a panic, moved through the duct into another room. The occupant of that room (another show attendee) joined our rescue team, but the cat kept going until it reached the very end of the wall of the Hotel.

No amount of coaxing and cajoling did any good and the owners began to insist that we tear down the wall.

"Let's try one more thing," I said and sent to the kitchen for six raw, smelly shrimp.

We removed the air conditioner and put the shrimp in the opening. With a bound, the cat leaped right into our Engineer's hands! There rose up a great cheer and the happy owners assigned the errant feline to its traveling box — just in case!

# I've got him by the collar

᷍ ᷍ ᷍ ᷍ ᷍ ᷍ ᷍ ᷍ ᷍

One day I was called to rescue a couple stuck on an elevator.

I immediately responded, expecting to find some sort of mechanical failure. What I discovered was a failure, all right, but hardly a mechanical one.

I forced the door open and discovered a calm man and his hysterical wife, clutching a dog leash that trailed up into the ceiling of the car. She was sobbing, "My dog...my dog..."

With horror, I surmised what must have happened and ran up the stairs to the floor above. Expecting a tragic scene, I was relieved to see a bewildered, but obviously unhurt poodle pressed against the elevator door. Within seconds, I cut the dog's leash and set it free.

Reuniting the poodle with its tearful mistress, I was puzzled by the husband's reaction. But, then I overheard him mumble to his wife: "This would never have happened if Fifi had slept in the kennel and I had slept in the bed!"

# A roaring good time

*We* have guests of all kinds. Never a dull moment. Many famous names have appeared on our guest register, but my favorite was Leo Lyon.

Leo came in with a roar...

Believe me, when he arrived, we all stood still. Stood still for fear we might be his main course. We watched to be sure he wasn't licking his chops. His trainer reassured us that he'd had dinner. But he might be looking for dessert!

You see, it wasn't a MAN named Leo Lyon. Our guest was a LION named Leo!

# New York, New York

$O$ur Hotel is in the heart of New York and we were filled to capacity. Every room was booked. It was snowing and festivities were in full swing in every ballroom.

One ballroom was the site of the Policeman's Ball. But, this was no ordinary Policeman's Ball. This was the Annual Gala of the Mounted Police. Their horses were housed in trailers outside.

Feeling sorry for his horse, one of the Mounties took the liberty of going out to the horse trailer and bringing his animal into the Hotel. Out of the cold. Somehow, he managed to sneak his horse through the lobby and up to his room on the 12th floor. Of course, the horse became restless. And started to gallop up and down the hallway. Security was called. The Chief of the Mounted Police was summoned. The Mountie was ordered to take his horse back to the trailer.

Now, try to picture yourself. Waiting for an elevator. In the world's most exciting city. In the lobby of an elegant, luxurious Hotel. The doors open and out steps a beautiful white horse. With a mounted policeman on its back.

Giddy Yap!

# He couldn't bear it

🐻 🐻 🐻 🐻 🐻 🐻 🐻 🐻 🐻

The circus was in town and all of the Hotel personnel were eagerly anticipating the arrival of the performers who were scheduled to stay with us.

The automatic sliding doors opened and in walked a famous circus celebrity. With his equally famous "Wrestling Bear." Much to our surprise, we were told that BOTH would be registered in the room!

A call came into to Room Service. The tray was prepared and a waiter dispatched to deliver it. He knocked on the door and announced himself. He was told to come in. When he entered the room, the guest was in the bathroom and yelled out to the waiter to please leave everything on the dresser. He would be right out to sign the check.

As the waiter walked into the room, he noticed the wrestling bear sitting on the bed. Their eyes met and the tray went flying! The waiter just couldn't BEAR it and fled the room!

# Llama Mama

*ⁱ ⁱ ⁱ ⁱ ⁱ ⁱ ⁱ ⁱ ⁱ*

*A* couple checked in, requesting two ground floor rooms. They asked if pets were allowed. The Front Desk Clerk assured them that family pets are always welcome at our Holiday Inn hotel, but cautioned that any damage done would be at the expense of the guest.

After completing their registration card, the couple retired to their rooms.

A quiet night passed.

The next morning, as they were leaving, the Housekeeping supervisor was shocked to see them leading two pet LLAMAS out to a trailer!

Much to everyone's amazement, no damage was found and the couple went on their way.

# Rroof! Rroof!

❧ ❧ ❧ ❧ ❧ ❧ ❧ ❧ ❧

*I*t was a windy, cold night and I was Manager on Duty. The Hotel was filled with all types of people, business men and women, families, pets, etc.

The Front Desk received a call. There was a dog barking on the second floor roof, above the pool area. I was paged. I went to the second floor. From the window in the vending area, I could see the little dog. To get to the dog, I had to climb out the window, in my dress and high heels.

I located the poor little puppy, which was cold and hungry. Cuddling him in my arms, my dress blowing upwards, my high heels slipping on the gravel roof, I struggled through the wind back to the window — which someone had closed!

I knocked and knocked. But no one came. The dog and I were stuck out on the roof. The minutes ticked past. My pager went off again, so I knew the Front Desk was looking for me.

Finally, through a crack in the curtains I saw the elevator doors open and a gentleman stepped off. I knocked and knocked, hoping he would let us in. The man looked around. Not seeing anyone, he started to walk away. The dog was struggling to get down. Hanging onto him, I knocked louder and finally the man walked over to the vending machine area. He pulled back the curtain and saw me standing there with the dog. He started laughing, opened the window, and took the dog from me. I gracefully climbed through the window, trying to hold my skirt down and keep my shoes on.

I explained the situation to the gentleman while taking the dog back into my arms. Thanking him, I had to laugh at my escapade as I carried the puppy down to the lobby.

# CHAPTER NINE

# *T*he Nature
## of Human
## Nature

ഇ ഇ ഇ ഇ ഇ ഇ ഇ ഇ ഇ ഇ

# The handicap space is between my ears

❧ ❧ ❧ ❧ ❧ ❧ ❧ ❧ ❧

*T*he Holiday Inn hotel was my weekday home for nearly three years while I worked for an important client. Whatever I might have expected, I never thought it would be a learning experience.

It all began when I walked to the indoor parking lot one morning. There was a ramp leading from the lot into the Hotel's Executive Offices. The parking space on one side of the ramp was larger than the others. And, that's where I liked to park my car. It was easier to drive in and out.

But, this time, a large, old station wagon was parked right behind my car. It was empty and the motor was running. I waited and waited. And waited. Five minutes went by. Seven minutes. My agitation grew. I had a job to get to and I did not want to be late.

Finally, an elderly gentleman emerged from the Hotel, hurried down the ramp and, with an apologetic smile, got into the station wagon. "Why didn't you park somewhere else?" I yelled. "Sorry," he replied and drove away.

I glared after him. There were plenty of empty spaces nearby. Why couldn't the fool have simply parked in one of them?!

This incident was repeated the following week and several times after that. Well, I was in a righteous rage. Why did he insist on parking right behind my car? Sure, I could have parked elsewhere. But, why should I give up my prized space just because this guy refused to use one of the empty spaces?

One morning, I had had enough. I climbed into his station wagon and backed it to the far end of the garage. There! Maybe that would make the point.

Two days later, there was the station wagon, right behind me again. I furiously waited for the man to return. After a couple of minutes, he hastened down the ramp to his car. I raged at him for inconveniencing a paying customer. He was making me late for an important meeting. WHY did he insist on parking right behind me!

"I'm really sorry," he said. "You see, I volunteered to drive some elderly ladies who live here to see their doctors. Most of them have trouble walking, so I park at the foot of this ramp and they don't have to go so far. As soon as they're comfortable, I come out and move my car."

"And, speaking of that," he continued, smiling again. "You really didn't have to move my car all the way to the far end, did you?"

Anyone who has suddenly come face to face with his own self-centeredness and egotistical assumptions will understand how I felt. It was a shock.

"No, I didn't," I stammered. "I'm the one who's really sorry."

From that moment on, I waited for the courtly gentleman who was helping to make the lives of a few elderly women easier to bear.

And, I waited contentedly.

# *May I see your driver's license, too?*

&a &a &a &a &a &a &a &a &a

*A*t 3:00 a.m. one night, a lady entered the lobby and marched straight to the Front Desk.

"May I help you?" inquired the desk clerk.

Pulling a gun and aiming it straight at him, she said, "I want all your cash — NOW!"

The nearby Night Auditor continued to post his figures and the cash register whined away, making enough noise to obscure any conversation behind him. Desperately, the clerk yelled his name. The auditor turned around, took in the situation, and froze.

At that moment, our night porter came into the Lobby with his hand on the pager in his pocket. Startled by his abrupt appearance, the "hold up" lady jerked the gun in his direction.

"Do you have a permit for that gun, lady?" he said with a surprising air of confidence. "If not, you're in real trouble!"

"Are you the security officer?" she asked.

"Put that gun away, right now!" demanded the porter.

The lady slowly looked at all three people in total disbelief, shoved the gun into her purse and ran out the door.

Hearts hammering, the three called the police and were relieved to learn a short time later that she was arrested at a nearby restaurant. And not because she didn't have a permit!

# Honesty is the best policy

≈ ≈ ≈ ≈ ≈ ≈ ≈ ≈ ≈

*E*arly last year I was sent to New York and stayed at the Holiday Inn Crowne Plaza on Broadway in Manhattan. I had been fortunate enough to obtain two tickets to see Phantom of the Opera and two for Aspects of Love.

In rushing to leave for a meeting, I left all four tickets sitting out on the desk. In plain sight. Tickets worth a small fortune.

During lunch, I realized my blunder. Knowing a little about the problems one can encounter in New York City, I kicked myself for being so stupid. I also wrote off the two shows.

Imagine my delight when I returned to the Hotel and found the tickets in an envelope with a note suggesting in the future I be more careful.

Thanks for the honesty and integrity, Holiday Inn Crowne Plaza!

# The lady doth protest too much

&a &a &a &a &a &a &a &a &a

*L*ocated near Mt. Rushmore, Yellowstone Park, and the Custer Battlefield, Sheridan, Wyoming is a popular tourist site throughout much of the year.

Upon being transferred to Sheridan as the General Manager, I was perplexed to find the Holiday Inn hotel lounge was suffering a decline in revenues at a time when our occupancy was up. Observing the casual, relaxed atmosphere of the area, I suspected the formal atmosphere of our lounge might be the problem. The staff dressed in tuxedo-type uniforms — complete with long black slacks, tux shirts and blouses, and bow ties. I wondered if a more casual uniform might help business.

The Bar Manager and I decided on a new uniform of polo shirts, walking shorts, and tennis shoes. But, when we announced the uniform change, two cocktail waitresses resigned in protest! We were shocked at their claim that the new uniforms were "too risque."

We went with the change, nevertheless, and business indeed improved.

From time to time, I wondered about the two waitresses, feeling a little guilty about having offended them. Thus, imagine my shock when our

Director of Food and Beverage walked into my
office one day, waving a "skin" magazine. Opened
to the centerfold. There was one of the indignant
waitresses and she wasn't wearing walking shorts
— or for that matter, anything else!

# *Happy Birthday!*

*I*'ve always found pleasure in being able to help our guests or just brighten their day. But, sometimes I feel our guests have taught me more in return.

I remember once, when I was waiting tables in our Hotel's restaurant, a group of three hearing-impaired ladies were seated in my section.

I was apprehensive when they indicated that they would rather try to speak instead of writing out their order, as many hearing-impaired people prefer to do. I misunderstood them and brought the wrong drinks. Twice. I was embarrassed and a little annoyed that they wouldn't make MY job easier by simply writing out their order on the pad I provided.

When one of the ladies left to use the restroom, the other two asked me to bring out a lit cake for her birthday. As she returned to her seat, I sneaked up behind her and presented the glowing cake. When I walked away, I thought I heard something like a soft cooing. I discreetly glanced into our mirror and saw the two women holding the other woman's hand and softly trying to sing "Happy Birthday." They seemed to be struggling so very hard to make each word as crystal clear as their speech training would allow to the lady who probably couldn't even hear their efforts.

I paused and marveled at the obvious warmth and intimacy the three very special women shared. As I felt my eyes welling up, I walked away.

# Take time to smell the roses

ða ða ða ða ða ða ða ða ða

*O*nce, many evenings ago at a Hotel far away, there was a chef who was indifferent to his job. Day in and day out, he labored in a kitchen filled with people who did their work with great joy and satisfaction. He envied his co-workers because they were happy with their jobs. He could not understand where such satisfaction came from...

But then he had occasion to discover that his job could only be as good as HE made it.

A young woman entered the Hotel restaurant one evening. She told her waitress that she was in quite a hurry and the waitress asked the chef to please prepare the meal quickly. The chef complied and later went into the restaurant to inquire if everything had been to the satisfaction of the diner. Just as the young woman paid her bill, she rose from the table, knocking her briefcase to the floor, spilling its contents. The chef helped her and initiated some idle conversation. She relaxed a bit, thanked him and departed.

Later that evening the chef thought about the incident and the nice young woman. He wondered if he should have told her to slow down, relax, enjoy her stay, smell the roses, or any of the many other proverbs about life. But then he thought, "How absurd! Me, a person of apathy trying to tell someone else how best to enjoy life!"

About ten days later, he received a nice note from the young woman. She was again thankful for the excellent meal and fine service, but this time she was also grateful for the chef's being a friend when she needed one. Anyone can cook a meal and anyone can serve a meal, but what really matters is that people get what they need, when they need it. At that place, at that time, she had needed a friend and the chef was lucky enough to be the one who was there for her.

For the first time, the chef was proud of the job he had done and would remind himself over the years that true job satisfaction comes with doing a good job and helping others do a good job.

# Braced for life

❦ ❦ ❦ ❦ ❦ ❦ ❦ ❦ ❦

Stubbornness is often thought of as a vice, but it can also be a virtue. Leslie is the perfect example.

I met her in February, 1986, while cleaning rooms at our Holiday Inn hotel in Philadelphia. My repeated knocks at the door of her room went unanswered, so I let myself in — surprised to find the room occupied.

"Please, come in," she protested as I offered to return later. She was engaged in a struggle with complex leg braces, the result of extensive surgery following an automobile accident.

I looked into her blue eyes and saw tears of real pain. "Let me help you," I urged. I could see the relief flood into her eyes as she lay back against the headboard. As I worked with the braces, I admonished her for trying to take them off by herself. She confessed that the choice had been entirely her own.

Earlier in the day, she had been released from the hospital. Unable to fly home to Miami for several months, she was assigned to a local nursing home for recuperation, against her wishes. So, the doctors had finally agreed to her staying at a hotel — provided she hire a private duty nurse.

That morning, Leslie followed the doctor's orders — to a point. She had taken a cab to the Hotel and was about to go straight to bed and await the arrival of the nurse. But, then, she changed her mind. After weeks of confinement, she wanted to "live" a little.

She directed the cab driver to take her to the "Whispering Wall" in Fairmont Park. When they arrived, she had the driver press his ear to one side while she spoke to him from the other end, 60 feet away. The acoustical qualities of the wall made their voices sound side-by-side.

Thrilled with life, Leslie asked the driver to make snowballs for her from the freshly fallen snow. He obliged only to find his efforts rewarded with a pelting from his passenger.

Finally, exhausted but happy, Leslie arrived at the Holiday Inn hotel and found the cheerless private duty nurse, impatiently waiting. The woman's dour face and uncompromising disposition put a damper on Leslie's high spirits. She scolded her for disobeying the doctor's orders.

"Who pays you?" asked Leslie. "Me or the doctor?"

"Why, you do," replied the woman, taken aback. "But, that's not the point."

"That is precisely the point," said Leslie, handing the nurse a $20 bill. "You're fired!"

I listened as she finished her account and said, "My mother used to warn me not to 'cut off my nose to spite my face.' You should have at least let her take the braces off — and then canned her!"

Leslie began to laugh, nodding in agreement. She laughed out of pure enjoyment of life and from the relief of knowing that soon she would be able to walk again. Her laugh was infectious and we both laughed so hard that it hurt.

Twice a year, Leslie returns to the Hotel for medical treatment and we savor our visits. We've kept in close touch and I always remind her about "noses" — the private joke we understand so well.

# Mama Jo

❧ ❧ ❧ ❧ ❧ ❧ ❧ ❧ ❧

$S$he has hundreds, maybe thousands, of children of all ages — from all walks of life. As I read the many letters and cards written through the past years to Mama Jo, I realize that this is a person loved by all who meet her. I watch the guests who frequent our Hotel repeatedly seek out this wonderful woman who brings a homelike feeling to those so far from home.

During Desert Storm, our Hotel became a military barracks for hundreds of men and women about to go to war. These brave soldiers were making their last stop before shipping overseas to an uncertain future.

It was early Sunday morning and troops filled the lobby, drinking one last cup of coffee. I turned to Mama Jo and said, "It's so quiet." I sensed that these brave men and women felt all alone.

Mama Jo and I looked at each other and we knew what was needed. Without a word, Mama Jo left the Front Desk and went around the lobby hugging each and every person "Good Bye." Before long, there wasn't a dry eye in the lobby.

Every day Mama Jo reaches out without thinking — just feeling. And, everyone knows she will be here, waiting for each and every one of them to return.

# They can fly, but they sure can't swim!

۶ ۶ ۶ ۶ ۶ ۶ ۶ ۶ ۶

*O*ver the years, I have seen many people, employees, and guests come and go. And, every person was a story in itself, but my all time favorite story is about a precision flying team...

About six years ago, we hosted the World Precision Flying Teams from eight different countries. We had a lot of fun talking with the different flyers from all around the world.

One of the Eastern European teams had an older KGB-type in charge. He was polite, but very demanding and always a little bit scary. One afternoon, he came running to our front desk and, in broken English, demanded directions to the nearest hospital!

We, of course, promptly complied and away he went. Our imaginations soared—had someone been tortured? Had someone been killed? What could have happened?

Later that afternoon, one of the guests on the English team came to the Front Desk. He was laughing so hard it took a few minutes to get the complete story. It seems two of our "precision" flyers dived into opposite ends of the swimming pool simultaneously. They swam straight into each other...breaking both their noses!

# Thanks, Mom!

੨ਡ ੨ਡ ੨ਡ ੨ਡ ੨ਡ ੨ਡ ੨ਡ ੨ਡ ੨ਡ

*I*n 1976, a widely known Hollywood celebrity came to stay with us. We were forewarned that she seldom patronized public restaurants because she ate only organically grown foods.

With the assistance of our Norwegian chef, we were determined to capture her favor. We succeeded in getting her to try our fresh water trout, brought to us daily from the icy mountain streams. We offered her limited selections of organically grown vegetables such as cucumbers, squash, and carrots.

But, after three days our creativity was exhausted. My 78-year old mother lives nearby and I asked her if she would help us. "Mom, just fix her a good wholesome meal," I said. At the appointed time, I picked up the prepared tray and personally delivered it to our guest. The dinner consisted of generous portions of fresh green beans, cream-style corn, cole slaw, fresh apples, and a generous portion of banana pudding.

In an interview with the local newspaper, just before leaving our area, the eccentric celebrity heaped praises on our staff and especially thanked the "chef" for the incredible health foods she had enjoyed at her last meal!

# My little blue spruce

❧ ❧ ❧ ❧ ❧ ❧ ❧ ❧ ❧

On a cold winter night, while working as the evening Hostess, I found a ladies purse. I was concerned about getting the purse back to its rightful owner, but did not feel comfortable going through someone else's purse to find identification. I called the Rooms Manager and had him come to the Hostess station. While he watched, I looked through the wallet for a name. The Front Desk confirmed that the "Littles" were registered guests. Mr. Little was notified and came down to the restaurant to retrieve his wife's purse.

When the Littles checked out the next morning, they left behind an envelope, addressed to me. Inside was a note thanking me for my honesty along with a $20 bill. While I appreciated their thoughtfulness, I did not feel I should be compensated for doing the "right" thing. But, I also did not want to risk offending these nice people by returning the money to them...

I wasn't sure what to do. And, then, it hit me! My husband and I are members of National Arbor Day Society and we order trees every year to plant on our land. Why not order two trees in the Littles' name! So, we did and I wrote Mrs. Little a note to let her know what I had done with the $20.00 and to tell her we named the two Colorado Blue Spruce trees "My Little Blue Spruce" in her honor.

I can only say that I am richer for having known the Littles and I will always remember that nice couple. There are two more beautiful trees growing taller every year..."My Little Blue Spruce!"

# Daughter-in-law in distress

≈ ≈ ≈ ≈ ≈ ≈ ≈ ≈ ≈

One afternoon, a guest left her dress with the bell stand to be sent out to the cleaners. At 5:00 p.m. she called to inquire when the dress would be returned to her. Unfortunately, we do not have same day service unless the item is in before 9:00 a.m. and we could not have her dressed cleaned and back to her that night. She asked to speak to the Manager on Duty.

I retrieved the dress from the bell stand and went to talk with the irate guest. Unfortunately, she was quite upset and did not want to talk. She snatched the dress from me and slammed the door!

Once back in my office, having regained my composure, I called and apologized for the inconvenience. I offered to help in any way I could. At this point, the guest started crying and wailed, "I am meeting my mother-in-law for the first time. I have nothing to wear. She already hates me. What am I going to do?"

I told her I would be right up. Armed with an iron and ironing board, I went back to her room. Together we looked through her clothes and agreed the crumpled dress was the best choice. While I pressed her dress, we exchanged a few mother-in-law stories and soon she was laughing.

Once in the freshly-pressed dress, however, she groaned as she looked in the mirror...her hair was a mess! I called for reinforcements. One of the Housekeepers gave her a hair style no mother-in-law could resist. Her makeover complete, we sent her on her way.

I checked on the young lady the next day, just to see how things had turned out. She was very excited and told me she was waiting for her new mother-in-law to pick her up to go shopping!

# A word about the illustrations

With the exception of the illustration on page 74, all drawings were provided by George L. Hoch, General Manager of the Holiday Inn-Ashley Plaza (Tampa, Florida).

Hoch began his affiliation with Holiday Inns, Inc. in 1982, as Resident Manager of the Holiday Inn on Biscayne Bay at Brickell Point in Miami, Florida. Interestingly enough, the hotel was one of several under Alias' direction at that time. However, the two hoteliers never met and were delighted to discover their shared backgrounds as they worked on completion of the book. Both were struck by the coincidence — "It is a small world, after all!"

With formal training in Hotel and Restaurant Administration (Florida State University B.S. in Business Administration as well as studies at the American College of Switzerland in Leysin), Hoch is occasionally recruited by his sales staff to illustrate flyers and promotional materials. Easily inspired by the humor of day-to-day situations, he finds himself frequently capturing the fun in whimsical cartoons. "I've always been a good doodler!" says Hoch.

The dollhouse drawing on page 74 was produced by Frank Cothran of Memphis, Tennessee. A graduate of Memphis State University with a Bachelor of Fine Arts degree, Cotham has done work for

such national publications as COSMOPOLITAN,
THE SATURDAY EVENING POST, and THE WALL
STREET JOURNAL.

# Contributors

We wish to thank Holiday Inn hotel employees and guests everywhere. Without them there would be no book. We especially thank the following individuals who shared their favorite memories and are the real "authors" of this endeavor.

Kay Alguire, HOLIDAY INN
McKinley, Texas

John Armstrong, HOLIDAY INN
Dover, Delaware

Jacqueline Bender, HOLIDAY INN
Altoona, Pennsylvania

Debi Bishop-Webber, HOLIDAY INN  CROWNE PLAZA
Los Angeles

Jean Ellen Bodin, HOLIDAY INN
Spring Lake, Michigan

Chad Boeddeker, HOLIDAY INN
Elgin, Illinois

Linda A. M. Bourque, HOLIDAY INN
Waterville, Maine

Melissa Brown, HOLIDAY INN NORTH
Fort Worth, Texas

Gary Burchett, HOLIDAY INN
Sheridan, Wyoming

Larry Burtchaell, HOLIDAY INN
North Platte, Nebraska

Norma J. Chumbley, HOLIDAY INN PARK
CENTRAL  Dallas, Texas

James A. Cooper, HOLIDAY INN
Cherokee, North Carolina

Laura B. Costello, HOLIDAY INN ARENA
Binghamton, New York

Walt Cunningham, HOLIDAY INN DOWNTOWN
St. Joseph, Missouri

Kathie Cyr, HOLIDAY INN DOWNTOWN
Hartford, Connecticut

Jennifer Davenport, HOLIDAY INN
South Plainfield, New Jersey

John P. Davey, HOLIDAY INN CROWNE PLAZA
Natick, Massachusetts

Donna Davidson, HOLIDAY INN
Dover, Delaware

Dick Dodge, PRIORITY CLUB MEMBER
Niagara Falls, New York

Joseph Dora, HOLIDAY INN HARBORSIDE
Kenosha, Wisconsin

Patricia Dominguez, HOLIDAY INN GEORGETOWN
Washington, D.C.

Sandy Douglas, HOLIDAY INN
Oil City, Pennsylvania

Annette Dreitzer, HOLIDAY INN JFK AIRPORT
Jamaica, New York

Linda Dukes, HOLIDAY INN EAST
Evansville, Indiana

David Dunn, HOLIDAY INN EAST
Evansville, Indiana

David Dykstra, HOLIDAY INN
Traverse City, Michigan

James Eckhardt, PRIORITY CLUB MEMBER
Toms River, New Jersey

Mary Eddy, HOLIDAY INN AIRPORT
San Antonio, Texas

Bonnie Ehlers, HOLIDAY INN
North Platte, Nebraska

Nancy Fannin, HOLIDAY INN
Waldorf, Maryland

Mary Farr, HOLIDAY INN
Pittsburgh, Pennsylvania

Randall Felts, HOLIDAY INN OVERTON SQUARE
Memphis, Tennessee

William Fieldman, PRIORITY CLUB
Brick, New Jersey

Debi Fierro, HOLIDAY INN PISCATAWAY
S. Plainfield, New Jersey

Tammy Figle, HOLIDAY INN
Bluefield, West Virginia

Donna Foley, HOLIDAY INN
Manhattan, Kansas

Joan Foster, HOLIDAY INN
Bartonsville, Pennsylvania

Grace Foust, HOLIDAY INN
Denton, Texas

Elie Fraiha, HOLIDAY INN CROWNE PLAZA
LAGUARDIA  New York City

Nancy Gallatin,  HOLIDAY INN
Kissimmee, Florida

Edwyna Sue Gordon, HOLIDAY INN
Waco, Texas

Denise Griffin, HOLIDAY INN CAPITAL BELTWAY
Lanham, Maryland

Phil Grosse, HOLIDAY INN CROWNE PLAZA
LAGUARDIA New York City

Alice Hahn, HOLIDAY INN
Bardstown, Kentucky

Dexter Hall, HOLIDAY INN UNION STATION
Indianapolis, Indiana

Thomas Healey, PRIORITY CLUB MEMBER
Cedar Grove, New Jersey

Paige Ann Hess, HOLIDAY INN
Appleton, Wisconsin

Thomas Hively,  HOLIDAY INN JACKSONVILLE
Orange Park, Florida

Carolyn Housley, HOLIDAY INN WORLD'S FAIR
Knoxville, Tennessee

Kevin Hughes, HOLIDAY INN
Ogallala, Nebraska

Mary Hughes, HOLIDAY INN INDEPENDENCE HALL
Philadelphia

Jerry Hurst, PRIORITY CLUB MEMBER
Milford, Michigan

John Husum, HOLIDAY INN EMERALD BEACH
Corpus Christi, Texas

Dorothy Hutson, HOLIDAY INN WEST
Milwaukee, Wisconsin

Joan Kendrick, HOLIDAY INN
Sweetwater, Texas

Mary Kiser, HOLIDAY INN
Biloxi, Mississippi

Irma Klimach, HOLIDAY INN PISCATAWAY. S.
Plainfield, New Jersey

Gail Koeune,  HOLIDAY INN ROLLING MEADOWS
Hawthorne Woods, IL

Ernest Vincent LaCour,   HOLIDAY INN BOARDWALK
Daytona Beach, FL

Robert N. Lawler, Jr.  PRIORITY CLUB MEMBER
Birmingham, Alabama

Harry Ledbetter.  HOLIDAY INN
Biloxi, Mississippi

Lydia Leong,  HOLIDAY INN METROTOWN
Burnaby,  B.C.

Elsie Lowery,  HOLIDAY INN
Florence, South Carolina

Barbara Mahler,  HOLIDAY INN GATEWAY
Eau Claire, Wisconsin

Carla Maneth,  HOLIDAY INN
Great Bend, Kansas

Marshall McCrea, III.,  PRIORITY CLUB MEMBER
Canonsburg, PA

Thelma McDonald,  HOLIDAY INN ON THE BAY
San Diego, California

Karen McEvoy,  HOLIDAY INN
Boise, Idaho

Marjie McSpadden,  HOLIDAY INN
Albuquerque, New Mexico

Michael Mulleady, HOLIDAY INN CONFERENCE
CENTER,  Willmar, MN

Charlie Nitschmann, HOLIDAY INN NORTH
Austin, Texas

William Nolan, HOLIDAY INN WATERFRONT
Portsmouth, Virginia

Tyrone O'Steen, HOLIDAY INN
Kingsland, Georgia

Susan Overfield, HOLIDAY INN
LaMarque, Texas

Judy Pazdernik, HOLIDAY INN
Detroit Lakes, Minnesota

Keith Pemberton, HOLIDAY INN UNION STATION
Indianapolis, Indiana

Ardis Pojar, HOLIDAY INN
Sioux City, Iowa

Kathy Powell, HOLIDAY INN WATERFRONT
Portsmouth, Virginia

Delia Quiroz, HOLIDAY INN ASHLEY PLAZA
Tampa, Florida

Ignacio Rangel, HOLIDAY INN NORTH
Newark, New Jersey

Beverly Saunders, HOLIDAY INN
Bluefield, West Virginia

Mike Seidenman, PRIORITY CLUB MEMBER.
Longmont, Colorado

Jamison Smith, HOLIDAY INN CHATEAU
Vail, Colorado

Jayne Steed, PRIORITY CLUB MEMBER
Wichita Falls, Texas

Diane Sumerlin, HOLIDAY INN
Chesapeake, Virginia

Kathy Thomas, HOLIDAY INN
Hollywood, California

Lyle P. Thomason, HOLIDAY INN
West Fargo, North Dakota

Theresa Thomas, HOLIDAY INN SOUTHEAST
Richmond, Virginia

Lisa Thompson, HOLIDAY INN
Biloxi, Mississippi

Linda Trautman,  HOLIDAY INN DOWNTOWN
St. Joseph, Missouri

Sheila Volk, HOLIDAY INN
Bluefield, West Virginia

Isobel Votaw, HOLIDAY INN
North Platte, Nebraska

Donald Wald, HOLIDAY INN
Yonkers, New York

Melissa Warner, HOLIDAY INN HARBORSIDE
Kenosha, Wisconsin

R. W. Willingham, HOLIDAY INN
Waycross, Georgia

# Afterword

I hope you have enjoyed reading *Without Reservations* as much as I enjoyed compiling it! These stories cover the range of human experience — from hilarious to heartwarming, powerful to poignant. Hoteliers are privileged to share people's lives on a daily basis and it was our intention to share this wealth of human experience with our readers.

When we first conceived this book we anticipated receiving funny stories — tales told and retold throughout our industry of folks locked out of their rooms, naughty nights behind closed doors, bartenders who have seen and heard it all.

Imagine our delight as day after day, stories from far and wide were delivered to our offices. Stories that made us laugh, stories that made us cry. We were overwhelmed at the breadth of emotions we experienced as we read these treasured memories of guests encountered by Holiday Inn hotel staff members. We came to realize that the most memorable of encounters were not always amusing. Often they were hilarious and we laughed so hard we cried as we read them, but sometimes we were so touched, tears of compassion flowed from our eyes.

We were especially touched by the story of Rick and a little girl's dollhouse. Here most surely was a young man who epitomized all that is good in humankind. With huge lumps in our throats, we all agreed that the story renewed our faith in humankind.

# *Order form*

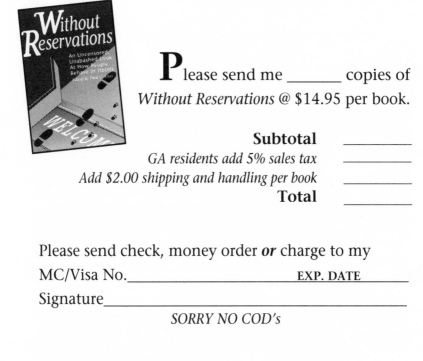

**P**lease send me _____ copies of
*Without Reservations* @ $14.95 per book.

|  |  |
|---|---|
| **Subtotal** | _____ |
| *GA residents add 5% sales tax* | _____ |
| *Add $2.00 shipping and handling per book* | _____ |
| **Total** | _____ |

Please send check, money order *or* charge to my

MC/Visa No._____ **EXP. DATE** _____

Signature_____

*SORRY NO COD's*

## *Ship to: (please print)*

Name _____

Street _____

City _____ State _____ Zip _____

Daytime Telephone No. _____

*Allow six weeks for delivery*

## *Mail order to:*

Sandcastles, Inc.
3340 Peachtree Road N.E., Ste. 1580
Atlanta, GA 30326
*or*
To FAX your order 24 hours a day call
1-404-233-8591

# Order form

**P**lease send me _____ copies of
*Without Reservations* @ $14.95 per book.

| | |
|---|---|
| **Subtotal** | _____ |
| *GA residents add 5% sales tax* | _____ |
| *Add $2.00 shipping and handling per book* | _____ |
| **Total** | _____ |

Please send check, money order *or* charge to my
MC/Visa No._____ **EXP. DATE** _____
Signature_____

*SORRY NO COD's*

## Ship to: (please print)

Name _____
Street _____
City _____ State _____ Zip _____
Daytime Telephone No. _____

*Allow six weeks for delivery*

## Mail order to:

Sandcastles, Inc.
3340 Peachtree Road N.E., Ste. 1580
Atlanta, GA 30326
*or*
To FAX your order 24 hours a day call
1-404-233-8591